HOMESTEADING

HAXTUN

AND THE

HIGH PLAINS

NORTHEASTERN COLORADO HISTORY

JEAN GRAY

THE History PRESS

Published by The History Press
Charleston, SC 29403
www.historypress.net

Front cover, bottom: *Homestead* (1994) by Jessie Whitney Scott. *Courtesy of Wayne and Doris Scott.*
Back cover, top: *Early Settlers* (1992) by Jessie Whitney Scott. *Courtesy of Wayne and Doris Scott.*

First published 2013

Manufactured in the United States

ISBN 978.1.60949.843.6

Library of Congress CIP data applied for.

Notice: The information in this book is true and complete to the best of our knowledge. It is offered without guarantee on the part of the author or The History Press. The author and The History Press disclaim all liability in connection with the use of this book.

CONTENTS

ACKNOWLEDGEMENTS

A history that goes back one hundred years depends on information that would be long gone if not for those who collect and preserve it for the future. This book depended much on those collectors. I am so grateful to the men and women of the Phillips, Fleming and Logan County Historical Societies who work vigorously to collect history for print and display. I especially want to thank Phillips County Museum volunteers Carol Haynes and Hilda Hassler for opening the museum on Wednesday afternoons and giving me access to the wealth of information stored there. Loads of thanks also go to Phillips County court clerk Joy Strack and Judy Beavers and other staff at the Phillips County Assessor's Office for digging through ancient files. I also owe a huge debt of gratitude to the late Alice (Taylor) Bamford for ensuring that fifty-six years of the *Haxtun Harvest* reside at the Phillips County Museum in Holyoke.

Many people provided letters, essays and photos that helped recreate this time in history. I am indebted to Randy Overstreet for allowing me to read the diary kept by his great-grandfather; to Virgil and Eloise Harms for entrusting me with Paoli's minute ledgers; to Wilbur Kipp for sharing his photos and memories; and to Reon Chaney for sharing his photos and memories and taking time to give me a driving history tour. Huge thanks go to Doris and Wayne Scott for visiting with me and permitting me to use a Jessie Scott print for the book's cover. Thanks to Wesley Brown for digging out his historic maps and scanning them for me; to the librarians at the Sterling Public Library, who found requested books either in the library or through inter-library loan and worked with me as I struggled to use the microfilm viewer; and to Linda Conn, librarian at the Fleming Library, for maintaining a wonderful local history section.

Others who provided information or photos included Tommy Thompson, Catalina Flores of *Palouse Magazine*, Alice Strohm descendants Connie Lawrence and DeLoris Fellers, CDOT librarian Joan Pinamont, Tom and Shawn Edwards, Irene Livingston, August and Jan Bjorklun, Ross Frank, Dewey and Lorraine Green, the Wisconsin Historical Society, Library of Earth Science librarian Naomi E. Herser, Alice Holloway, John M. Delander descendants Marguerite Baker and Scott Williams, Rebekka (Syed) Jackson, Ezekiel Scott descendants Critia Hadley and Lisa Betz, Larry and Mary Unrein, Wayne Wertz and Darlene Bornhoft.

A special thanks to Gay McDaniel and Dorothy Ortner for taking the time to read the manuscript with red pen in hand, to Becky LeJeune and Katie Orlando of The History Press for fielding my numerous questions and to Julia Turner of The History Press for her excellent editing skills.

The two prints for the cover of this book were painted by Jessie (Whitney) Scott. Scott moved with her family to Dailey, Colorado, from Portis, Kansas, shortly after her birth and developed her love of art at an early age. She began to draw after viewing Pikes Peak from a train window when she was four years old. She specialized in western landscapes, and her painting *Mountain Mist* hung in the Agricultural Hall of Fame in Kansas City, Kansas. She was a prolific artist who worked in oils, watercolor, sculpture, stained glass and, as her eyesight failed in her later years, ceramic tiles, working well into her nineties. Her murals hang in area banks, and her stained-glass windows adorn area churches. Those she created for her own church, the Haxtun Church of the Brethren, depict the life of Christ from his birth to his Ascension. Jessie Scott's paintings can be found in private collections throughout the United States and Europe. Her amazing body of work is a source of pride for Northeast Colorado.

FOREWORD

This book represents Jean Gray's passion for the subject and the numerous hours she spent researching the history of this special place in the state of Colorado.

The pioneers of this area showed great faith, perseverance and determination. They saw something special here that gave them the hope and dedication to establish the area into a place loved by those who call it home.

When this community settles on a goal, many pitch in to complete that goal in a successful way, not always without bumps and hurdles to cross, but with determination, dedication and hard work they accomplish the mission.

The men and women who homesteaded this area left an enduring mark. This history points out the many times that these settlers supported each other, a trait that continues today. Those who lived through rigorous times fought their way to success and prominence in a variety of fields and left their imprints on this part of northeast Colorado.

This book is long overdue, and I tip my hat to Jean Gray for telling this story.

GAY MCDANIEL
Mayor of Haxtun
Colorado 1992–2008

Chapter One

PRAIRIE, INDIANS AND BUFFALO

Ice ages, tropical oceans, volcanic eruptions and ascending ancient layers of earth designed the 104,247 square miles that became Colorado with three geological landscapes: the plateaus of the Western Slope, the central mountain region and the eastern High Plains. Of the High Plains, Walt Whitman wrote in 1883: "I wonder indeed if the people of this continental West know how much of first-class art they have in these prairies—how original and all your own—how much of the influences of a character for your future humanity, broad, patriotic and new?"

On the prairie that Whitman describes, the history of Haxtun and the farmlands surrounding it and its neighboring communities—Paoli, Dailey and Fleming—emerged. The four towns lie along a twenty-two-mile stretch of Colorado's U.S. Highway 6, with Haxtun and Paoli in Phillips County to the east and Dailey and Fleming in Logan County to the west.

Colorado is a semiarid state with an average annual precipitation of between six and sixty inches of moisture from snow and rain, depending on altitude and location. Areas at fourteen thousand feet receive five times as much precipitation as those at altitudes below five thousand feet, which include the eastern plains.

The High Plains, which lie within a larger area known as the Great Plains, stretch from the base of the Rocky Mountains east to the western edge of Nebraska, south to the Texas Panhandle and north to South Dakota. Early explorers to the area found grassland filled with buffalo and Indians, a barren country with minimal water and few trees. Zebulon Pike, after exploring the Great Plains for President Thomas Jefferson in 1806, named it the Great American Desert. Major Stephen Long, who followed Pike with an expedition in 1820, entered Colorado near Julesburg, some forty miles northeast of Haxtun, and followed the Platte River to Colorado Springs. He declared the prairie east of the Rocky Mountains "almost wholly unfit for cultivation." One hundred years later, a group of hardy individuals would prove Long wrong, but the first humans to enter the area came to hunt.

Prehistoric people came to the High Plains well after the ice age summer (when temperatures remained too cold to melt the snow and ice) that began over sixteen thousand years ago and after the dinosaurs, mammoths, mastodons, camelops, giant bison antiquus, camels, giant sloths and cheetahs that had wandered the grasslands foraging food during that time. Archaeological digs and artifact discoveries, including a 1985 Phillips County discovery by Virginia Pfau, show that several cultures of prehistoric people hunted in the area. The *Holyoke Enterprise* reported an archaeologist's conclusion that "the Paleo-Indian period projectile," found by Pfau, belonged to the "Hell Gap period" of about eight thousand to nine thousand BC.

Fifty-four years before Pfau's dig, on August 24, 1931, the *Holyoke State Herald* reported that W.M. Lytle of Julesburg discovered skeletal remains of ancient people along with stone and flint implements and weapons, pottery and bones of animals.

In 1987, anthropologist Dr. Elizabeth A. Morris, PhD, and ten Colorado State University (CSU) students dug arrowheads, spearheads, knives, scrapers, large animal skeletons, hearths and pottery pieces from Schlachter Farms, eleven and one-half miles east of Haxtun. "The site is on a hilltop with a nearby water source making it a preferred campsite for prehistoric hunters and travelers," wrote Dr. Morris. A display, constructed by student Roger Falk, a 1984 Haxtun High School graduate and son of Patricia "Tish" and Wayne "Jack" Falk, remains at the Phillips County Museum in Holyoke. The museum displays hundreds of Native American artifacts contributed by area residents.

Dr. Morris speculated that prehistoric Indians lived in the area when "herds of buffalo and antelope wandered freely." The site, which represented Indian hunting camps dating from around 1 AD to 1700 AD, netted thirty-four projectile points from Late Archaic, Plains Woodland, Republican and Dismal River cultures.

The Late Archaic period artifacts included tipped spears or atlatl darts dating back seven thousand years. The atlatl, a wooden throwing stick, allowed the hunter to propel the spear or dart harder and farther by

This display created by Roger Falk at the Phillips County Museum in Holyoke shows items from a 1987 archaeological dig at the Schlachter Farms east of Haxtun by anthropologist Dr. Elizabeth A. Morris, PhD, and a team of ten Colorado State University students. The dig netted arrowheads, spearheads, knives, scrapers, large animal skeletons, hearths and pottery pieces. *Author photo.*

extending the length of the arm. Late Archaic period people lived in rock shelters but roamed the plains gathering and hunting food.

The Plains Woodland or Ceramic period, which began around 1 AD, introduced cord-wrapped pottery, smaller projectile points and the use of the bow and arrow. From 1000 to 1400 AD, the Upper Republican culture occupied the same valley as the Woodland people. "These Indians probably sought buffalo to hunt as their preferred meat source," wrote Dr. Morris.

The Dismal River culture surfaced between 1500 and 1725 AD. These hunter-gatherers, ancestors of the Apache, lived in villages and created a distinct pottery. The Woodland and Upper Republican cultures lived mostly in the east, and the Dismal River culture lived farther west toward the foothills of the Rocky Mountains; but it was about this time that the eastern Colorado and western Kansas Indians started riding horses brought by Spanish explorers, allowing these cultures to lead a nomadic lifestyle. "Horses changed the peaceful farmers and hunters into rapidly moving raiders, who not only hunted buffalo more effectively but who also competed

The Phillips County Museum's Native American collection includes numerous arrowheads, knives, baskets and clothing. *Author photo.*

with each other, with young warriors counting 'coup' on each other for honor in actual battle," wrote Dr. Morris. "However, it is thought that the blood-thirsty fighters opposing soldiers and pioneers on the western frontier were not so warlike before their lands and their buffalo hunting lifestyle were seriously threatened."

The Indians probably encountered white explorers on Colorado's eastern plains as early as the eighteenth century, as indicated by carvings on two limestone slabs uncovered in the late 1940s. A *Denver Rocky Mountain News* story reported that the date—June 20, 1787—carved into the stones offered "the first on-the-spot evidence that there were white men in Colorado that early." State historian Dr. LeRoy R. Hafen theorized that a French frontiersman had carved the date. Searchers found an arrowhead nearby as well as buffalo bones and spots of burnt rock, indicating a campfire. Fred Johnson found the stones on land he leased from Leonard Sharpe while helping his dog dig a jackrabbit from its burrow south of Haxtun.

When settlers came to Colorado in the late nineteenth century, they found three principal tribes of Indians, according to Hafen and Hafen's *Colorado Story*. The short, stocky, dark-skinned Utes, called the "black Indians," lived in the mountains. The Arapahoe (meaning "tattooed on the breast"), taller than the Utes and lighter skinned, wandered the prairie between the upper waters of the Arkansas and Platte Rivers. The Cheyenne first settled in South Dakota but, by 1800, had moved southward onto the Great Plains, where they rode horses, adapted to the roving life and became friends with the Arapahoe.

Other Colorado tribes included the Comanche, Kiowa, Apache, Sioux, Pawnee and Shoshone. The Comanche lived on the eastern plains of Colorado until 1830, when the Arapaho and Cheyenne pushed them south of the Arkansas River. Close allies with the Cheyenne, the Arapaho wintered in the Rocky Mountains but traveled to the plains to hunt buffalo during spring birthing season and fall rutting season. The Sioux lived mainly in Wyoming and the Dakotas but followed the buffalo. The Cheyenne came to Colorado soon after the Arapaho, settled on the plains and often banded with the Arapaho to fight the Comanche, Kiowa, Shoshone and Ute tribes. The Pawnee lived in Nebraska but hunted buffalo on the eastern plains of Colorado.

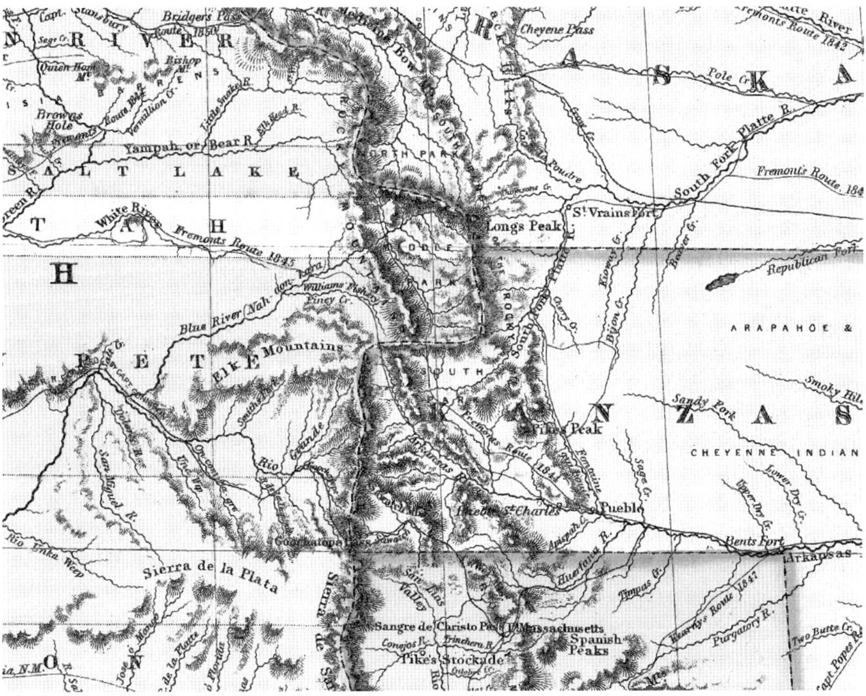

As shown in this 1861 J.H. Colton map, the northeast portion of Colorado, from the fortieth parallel (Baseline Road in Boulder) and east of the Continental Divide was in Nebraska Territory, while much of the rest of eastern Colorado was in Kansas Territory. *Courtesy of Wesley Brown.*

The United States acquired Colorado in three sections: the eastern plains as part of the 1803 Louisiana Purchase; the western portion from Mexico in 1848; and the remainder from the Republic of Texas in 1850.

When Congress passed the Kansas-Nebraska Act in 1854, granting territories authority over slavery, much of present-day Colorado, including Pike's Peak in the Rocky Mountains and a large portion of the southeastern plains, lay in the Kansas Territory. The northeastern corner of Colorado lay in the southwest corner of the Nebraska Territory. Both areas, as well as parts of New Mexico and Utah, became the Colorado Territory when Congress created it on February 28, 1861.

The first Colorado Territorial Legislature met on September 9, 1861, and divided the territory into seventeen counties: Arapahoe, Boulder, Clear Creek, Conejos, Costilla, Douglas, El Paso, Fremont, Gilpin, Huerfano, Jefferson, Lake, Larimer, Park, Pueblo, Summit and Weld. Weld covered the northeast corner while the remaining sixteen counties spread over the remainder of the Colorado Territory. The Leavenworth to Pike's Peak Express crossed Weld County and led to the gold fields. A number of forts and Indian trading posts sprang up along the trail, including Fort Sedgwick—a headquarters for troops ordered to protect communications and trade routes from hostile Indians—and the Julesburg trading post named after Jules Beni—a Frenchman known as "Old Jules."

Jules Beni ran his trading post while serving as a stage keeper for an overland stage company. Sweetwater division agent Jack Slade shot Jules to

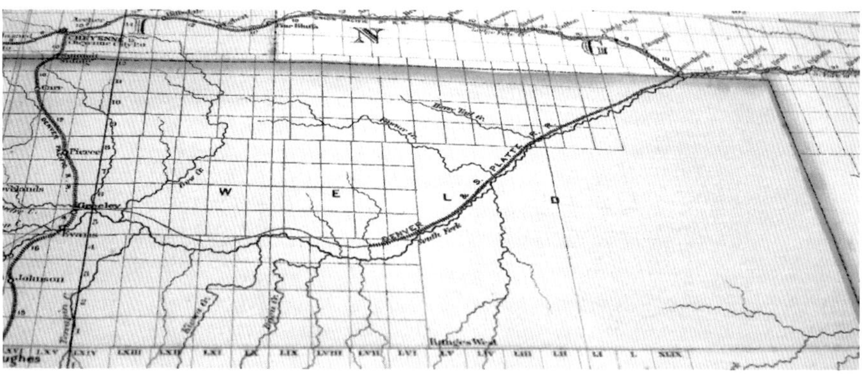

This 1873 Asher & Adams Weld County map shows the unsettled land that later became Logan County and then Sedgwick and Phillips Counties. The map shows only one railroad line entering northeastern Colorado at Julesburg. The map is from the *Asher & Adams New Topographical Atlas and Gazetteer* of New York. The solid black lines indicate railroad lines. *Courtesy of Wesley Brown.*

death in Julesburg in 1861 during a feud over mail tampering charges by the stage company. A hearing in Fort Laramie ruled the killing a "legal execution."

Julesburg was first located below the South Platte River east of where Lodgepole Creek enters from the north. Pony Express riders changed horses at this site in 1860–61. The cavalry arrived in 1864, setting up camp at Julesburg before moving one mile west to Camp Rankin, later named Fort Sedgwick. On November 29, 1864, seven hundred members of the Colorado Volunteer Militia, led by John Chivington, attacked a village of Cheyenne and Arapaho encamped at Sand Creek in southeastern Colorado, killing and mutilating over one hundred Indians, including women and children. The attack angered the Indians and led to the January 1865 plunder of the station and supply store at Julesburg, the killing of a number of soldiers at Fort Sedgwick and the destruction of stations and emigrant trains. In a second attack in February, the Indians burned Julesburg to the ground and destroyed telegraph lines. In mid-July, the Indians attacked stations and freight trains between Julesburg and Fort Morgan. They burned buildings, ran off livestock and killed a number of men.

The second Julesburg, located four miles east of the original town site near the Fort Sedgwick Military Reservation, remained until June 1867, when the Union Pacific Railroad arrived. The third Julesburg site, later named Weir, served as a shipping point, while gaining a reputation as the "wickedest City in the West."

Emma Burke Conklin, in *A Brief History of Logan County*, reported that six thousand people lived in and around Julesburg at one time. J.M. Weir, whose father came to Julesburg in 1867, described it as a "notorious place, a town of tents and shanties, whither drifted and lodged the most reckless gang of outlaws that ever congregated at any one point in the western frontier." The site of the third Julesburg remained busy until the Union Pacific opened a branch line to Denver and set up a junction at a new town site several miles east on July 2, 1884. Locals opted to keep the name Julesburg and incorporated in 1886.

In 1868, Indians pillaged western Kansas, and on September 16, Colonel James W. Forsyth and a small force of fifty-one scouts tracked the Cheyenne Dog Soldiers and Sioux to a camp in the Valley of the Arickaree, a branch of the Republican River near the eastern border of Colorado about fifteen miles south of Wray.

In Forsyth's version reported in E.S. Sutton's *Southwest Nebraska and the Republican River Valley Tributaries*, the Indians encountered the soldiers, who were riding through the narrow gorge, and the white men fired on the

The collection of Native American artifacts at the Phillips County Museum in Holyoke includes this display of pottery and grinding stones that early settlers discovered in the area and donated to the museum. *Author photo.*

Indians, driving them back. However, Starving Elk, one of the Cheyenne warriors, said the scouts retreated to a small island in the middle of the streambed without firing a shot and dug rifle pits in the sand to prepare for a fight. Forsyth mistakenly thought he was being attacked by a large number of Indians, but actually, most remained at the village on Black Wolf Creek. One Indian died in the initial attack that killed most of the scouts' horses. By the next morning, "half of Forsyth's men lay dead or wounded; they had no food except raw horse flesh."

Forsyth's first lieutenant, Frederick Henry Beecher, was among the dead, and Forsyth himself was severely injured. The Indians held off, waiting for the scouts to perish, believing that no help would come. They were mistaken. Forsyth made three attempts to send men to Fort Wallace for help; two returned unsuccessful, but the third, Colonel Louis H. Carpenter, came back on the ninth day followed by the Buffalo Soldiers of the Tenth U.S. Cavalry. When the cavalry arrived, the Indians disappeared.

The final Indian battle on Colorado's eastern plains followed another western Kansas raid. The Battle of Summit Springs took place on July 11, 1869, when General Eugene A. Carr, three hundred men from the Fifth Cavalry and a battalion of Pawnee scouts rode into the Cheyenne Dog

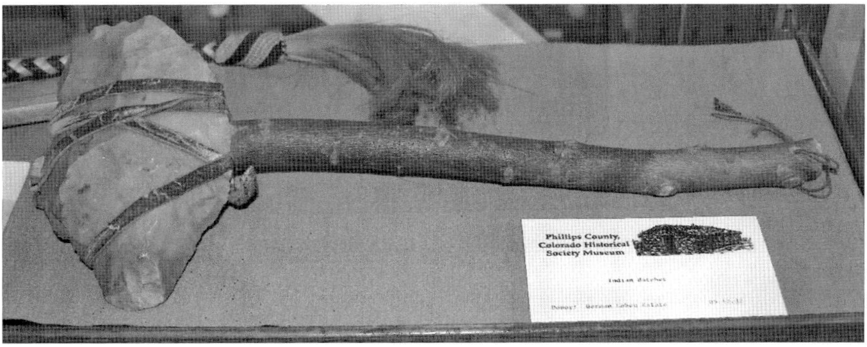

The Phillips County Museum in Holyoke displays hundreds of Native American artifacts found in the area, including this hatchet donated by the Herman Leben Estate in 1932. *Author photo.*

Soldiers' camp near Sterling. The Dog Soldiers held two white women that they had captured near Lincoln, Kansas, the previous May. Following the battle, in which fifty-two Cheyenne—including Tall Bull—died, the soldiers found both women but saved only one. Twenty-eight-year-old Susanna Alderdice, who had watched her four children die at the hands of the Cheyenne, died from a tomahawk wound to the head inflicted by one of Tall Bull's squaws. Tall Bull shot twenty-year-old Maria Weichel, whose husband the Indians had also killed, but she recovered from her wound and lived to tell of the torture and abuse the two women endured.

WHERE THE BUFFALO ROAMED

A party of men led by explorer Juan De Oñate in 1599 found the Plains Indians "numerous" and living in "rancherías" made from tanned buffalo hides that they moved to follow the buffalo. In his book, the *Hunting of the Buffalo*, E. Douglas Branch described the migratory habits of the buffalo. "Often many small herds assimilated into one herd of ten thousand or ten million," with a seasonal migration from 250 to 400 miles in length. Rutting season lasted from early July to late September. During this time, small herds gathered in a dense mass, and the "roaring and running, bellowing and tramping," could be heard two or three miles away. Then, "at the end of the rutting season, the great herd gradually resolved itself into little foraging bands again."

In 1832, Congress declared "Indian Country a legal entity," and forbade "any white person" without license from the Indian Commission to set foot in the "permanent" home of the American Indian. However, that failed to stop the migration of freighters, bullwhackers, miners, schooners and settlers that ventured onto the Great Plains. The buffalo hunters came too, and by 1837, they had glutted the buffalo robe market so much that a surplus of 23,000 robes carried over to the next season. By 1843–44, no market remained and neither did the boundless buffalo herds.

While the fur trade took its toll, the building of the railroad and military intervention changed tradition for the buffalo and the Indians. The railroad divided the buffalo into two herds. The northern herd of about one million grazed the Powder River country, and the southwest herd roamed from Texas north to the plains along the Republican between the Arkansas and South Platte rivers. In 1868, pleasure seekers found that the railroad opened up a new way to "satisfy their thirst for blood," wrote Branch. The ten-dollar round-trip railway excursion and buffalo hunt allowed participants to ride the train and shoot buffalo along the way. Officials hired Buffalo Bill Cody, who killed 4,280 buffalo in eighteen months, to provide buffalo meat to feed the construction crew. He also served as guide for one of the largest military junkets of that time.

One of the participants, Henry Eugene Davies, gave a first-person account of the hunt in *Ten Days on the Plains*, a book he privately printed in a limited edition in 1872. In the 1985 reprint of the book, editor Paul Andrew Hutton wrote: "Covering almost two hundred miles in ten days, Davies and his companions left a trail of empty champagne bottles and animal carcasses from Fort McPherson, Nebraska, to Fort Hays, Kansas. Over 600 buffalo were slaughtered, along with hundreds of elk, antelope and wild turkey before the junket was over." Davies describes "the wanton slaughter of western wildlife and unconsciously exposes the part played by the army in this environmental disaster," wrote Hutton. The expedition followed a policy initiated by its host, Lieutenant General Philip Henry Sheridan, of "exterminating the buffalo as a way of destroying the economic base of the Plains Indians." Although the excursion was one of the largest, it was not the only one.

In 1872–73, a time when there were more buffalo hunters on the plains than ever before or afterward, three western railroads shipped about 1,250,000 buffalo skins. The largest buffalo-skin tannery ever built was located in Greeley.

This slaughter might have spelled the extinction of the American buffalo except for the efforts of a man named Scotty Philip. Philip, a native of

Buster, a two-thousand-pound bull buffalo, shows off for the camera as he heads for a spot in the fence at his home in Phillips County. Local farmer Paul Mailander purchased Buster and a herd of five heifers at the National Western Stock Show and plans to raise the animals for the health benefits of the meat. He expects to release the animals into a pasture this summer where they will be grass fed. Although the buffalo no longer roam free on the prairie, they remain undomesticated and aggressive. *Author photo.*

Scotland, migrated to Indian country in the Black Hills of South Dakota from Victoria, Kansas, in September 1875 at age seventeen. In his book *Scotty Philip: The Man Who Saved The Buffalo*, Wayne C. Lee wrote of Scotty Philip's adventures as he sought his fortune, first in gold and later in land. Scotty Philip, who settled on a ranch north of Fort Pierre, South Dakota, and served in the South Dakota Senate, saw his first picture of a buffalo as a boy in Scotland and admired the "huge shaggy animals." He felt that such a monarch deserved a better fate than the hide hunters had given it, so after discovering a herd on the range along the Cheyenne River, he brought them back to his ranch. The herd of fifty-seven buffalo grew, and at the time of Philip's death in 1906, his herd numbered about one thousand. Most of the buffalo in parks and reserves across the West today are descended from Scotty's herd.

One of the last reported sightings of buffalo in northeastern Colorado occurred in November 1929, when the *Haxtun Harvest* reported that an escaped herd of between forty to fifty buffalo from a Sterling preserve delayed an eastbound train.

Policy Changes Open High Plains to Homesteaders

Two 1871 developments opened eastern Colorado for settlement. First, the United States passed an act that declared that "thereafter no tribe within the territory of the United States should be recognized as a power entitled to make treaties with the United States," and second, a man named Columbus Delano became Secretary of the Interior. Delano dedicated himself to "opening the whole of the Great Plains to the western farmers" who "wanted that land."

Delano's predecessor, J.D. Cox, followed an Indian-friendly policy that Delano proclaimed he was "done with." He suggested that the estimated 240,000 Indians living in the West be removed in order to release 93,692,731 acres of land to farmers, the "bone and sinew of the nation." He encouraged the elimination of the buffalo, and thus the "Indians' mode of life would become a myth." He predicted that given the choice between the Great Plains and starvation or the Indian Territory and agriculture, the Indians would choose the latter.

The Indians traveled to Washington where Red Cloud, chief of the Oglala Lakota (Sioux), told President Ulysses S. Grant that he only wanted to keep the "little spot I have left." He also went to Delano asking him to stop the white men from settling in Indian country and driving off the game. Delano responded with non-commitment. A few in Congress fought the policy, but most sided with Delano.

The flesh and tissues of buffalo carcasses rotted on the ground between the Platte and Republican Rivers, leaving white, bare skeletons as homesteaders arrived. In the lean years of the 1870s, they gathered the buffalo bones and took them to the nearest railroad station. The bones, used in refining sugar and making fertilizer and fine bone china, brought between $2.50 and $15.00 per ton.

Two months after the creation of the Colorado Territory, the southern states seceded from the Union, and the Civil War began. Although Colorado had settlers with divided sympathies, the legislature pledged the territory as part of the Union. The people ratified the Colorado Constitution on July 1, 1876, the one-hundredth anniversary of American Independence, giving it the nickname the "Centennial State." One month later, President Grant proclaimed Colorado the thirty-eighth state. That same year, Alexander Bell rang his first telephone.

In 1887, as homesteaders began to fill the area, the Colorado legislature created Logan and Washington Counties from the eastern

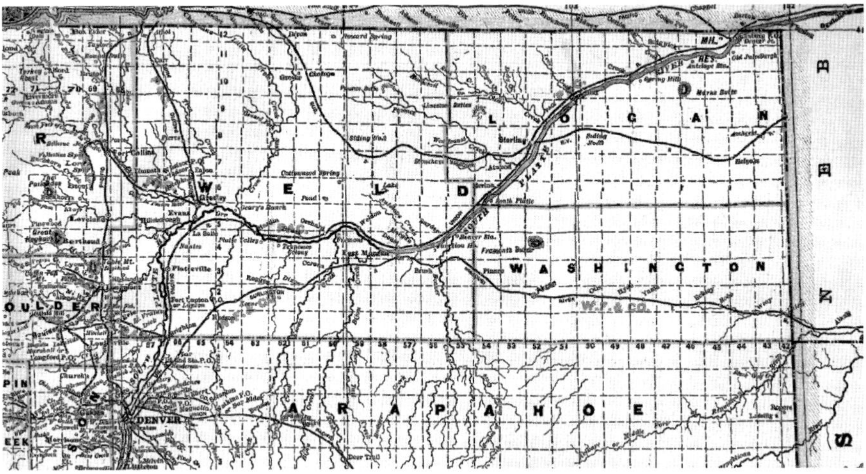

In 1887, the Colorado legislature created Logan and Washington Counties from the eastern half of Weld County as shown in this map produced by George F. Cram of Chicago, Illinois, one of the major map publishers of the late nineteenth century. By this time, three railroad lines crossed northeastern Colorado. *Courtesy of Wesley Brown.*

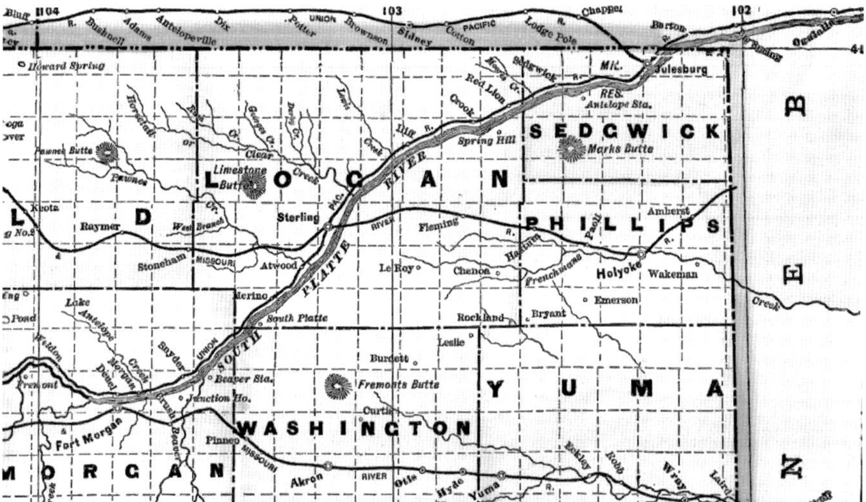

The Colorado legislature carved Sedgwick and Phillips Counties from the eastern portion of Logan County as shown in this 1889 edition of the *New General Atlas* by the William Bradley & Brothers Company of Philadelphia, Pennsylvania. *Courtesy of Wesley Brown.*

half of Weld County. Then, two years later in 1889, it created Sedgwick and Phillips Counties from the eastern portion of Logan County. Officials named Logan County for General John A. Logan, who fought in both the Mexican-American War and for the Union in the Civil War before entering politics. Phillips County namesake R.O. Phillips served as secretary of the Lincoln Land Company.

Chapter Two

CATTLE, COWBOYS, RAILROADS AND HOMESTEADS

The cattle industry in Colorado happened by chance. When a December 1864 storm overtook a wagon train heading to Camp Douglas, Utah, the sojourners were compelled to set up quarters for the winter. They turned their cattle loose, expecting them to perish, but instead, the animals remained nearby, feeding on the dried grass as snow and cold blew around the camp. When spring arrived, the campers found the cattle in better condition than when they had turned them out four months previously.

With the massive herds of buffalo gone, the stock industry, with its cattle kings and bronco-riding cowboys, grew rapidly across eastern Colorado's abundant government land with scant farming. The first cowboys came from Mexico, but as their reputation as courageous, daring and reckless figures spread, many adventurous young Americans headed West to join them. When the Andrew M. Axelson family arrived to homestead near Haxtun in 1885, they found cowboys of mixed breeds: "Some weather beaten, reckless and gun happy; some reliable; others green with fancy boots, silver spurs and pearl handled revolvers."

Open range allowed the cattle to roam for miles over the plains, necessitating a roundup season that began with branding in July or August and lasted until the cattle shipped east in the autumn. A Logan County cowboy, quoted in Conklin's *A Brief History of Logan County*, described the roundup: "There would be fifteen to eighteen wagons with about twenty men to each wagon. As they broke camp in the morning and started out the day's work, there would be four hundred mounted men, making a striking picture, reminding one of some great army movement."

Chuck time at a roundup in Logan County sometime in the late 1880s. *Courtesy of Reon Chaney.*

Emerson Hough characterized the cowboy as a misrepresented western legend: "They remember the wild momentary freaks of the man, but forget his lifetime of hard work and patient faithfulness. The way in which we should look at the cowboy of the passing West is not as a curiosity, but as a product; not as an eccentric driver of horned cattle, but as a man suited to his times."

Hafen's *Colorado Story* described the reality: "He was in the saddle from daylight to dark for months at a time, drinking filthy water from shallow water holes, breathing thick dust from wheeling herds, straining patience with footsore doggies, curbing the will of stubborn steers. He was so tired by night time that he forgot the bumps under his blanket and the hardness of his pillow."

Not all cowboys worked for an honest wage. Some turned to rustling (stealing cattle), a crime that plagued eastern Colorado ranchers during the 1890s. The cattlemen fought back with the formation of the Cattle and Horse Protective Association on February 4, 1899, and on May 29, 1903, *Ranch and Range Magazine* reported a possible end to the problem: "With the sending to the State Penitentiary of two convicted Yuma County cattle rustlers, and the killing of another who was shot by a Negro in a saloon brawl in Omaha [Nebraska], the rustler gang in eastern Colorado has been broken up." The magazine credited Judge Granville Pendleton, later district attorney for northeastern Colorado's Thirteenth Judicial District, with sending more than "three score to the penitentiary."

Stampedes offered another concern for the open range cowboy as related in the *Logan County Ledger*. One night in 1896, as Fleming pioneer Ed Morris and three other cowboys guarded about one thousand head of cattle, a thunderstorm came up: "A sharp streak of lightning and a terrible clap of thunder brought every hoof up and running south. We didn't know anything about the lay of the land, but found out very soon that it was full of draws and very rough. We finally all got on the left side of the herd and by shooting our six-shooters down close to the leaders, we got them milling and finally got them quieted down." The relief guard found them the next morning, several miles from where the stampede began.

The cowboys enjoyed celebrating after a hard day in the saddle, and Ed Morris recalled a time when he and a couple other cowboys rode into Sterling for some fun: "Sterling was just a cow town and Front Street was wild and wicked. We stayed a little too long and when we got ready to leave, we decided to wake up the town. Rather than go down the street, we rode down the board walk on a high lope shooting out the coal oil lights along the way." Ed Morris farmed and ranched, along with selling Dodge and Overland automobiles, until he retired at Fleming in 1963. He died there on April 1, 1968.

When Edward Anderson arrived in Colorado from Sweden through Nebraska with his son Sigfred in 1886, he filed a claim twelve miles northeast of Haxtun. The remaining ten members of the family arrived in 1887. Edward and Sigfred took jobs working for the railroad, but son Albert became one of the last open range cowboys in the area, riding as far east as Holyoke for a rancher who ran cattle from Brush to Sterling.

John W. Iliff, one of the earliest cattle kings in Colorado, established headquarters at what later became the town of Iliff along the South Platte River twelve miles northeast of Sterling. Iliff drove thousands of cattle from Texas, grazed them for a year or two and then shipped them east on the Union Pacific Railroad. When he died in 1876 at age forty-six, his cattle holdings were so large that he could travel from Julesburg to Greeley and always sleep and eat at one of his ranches.

In 1900, Ab Fleming, who came to Phillips County in 1886, and Holyoke physician Dr. M. Smith became partners in a cattle business, setting up headquarters twelve miles northeast of Haxtun in Sedgwick County. Around five thousand cattle owned by the ranch roamed as far north as the South Platte River, and cowboys used one hundred horses to herd them. The two sealed a partnership that lasted twenty-four years with a handshake. When Ab Fleming died in 1934, the *Harvest* wrote, "So far as can be learned, there was never a disagreement between the two. They were bound only by their spoken words, which apparently were never forgotten or misconstrued." Dr. Smith had died a few years before Fleming.

In 1901, David and Albertine Templeton, called Uncle Davy and Aunt Tille by friends and family, founded their ranch nine miles northwest of Haxtun. The Templeton Ranch became one of the largest in the state, with hundreds of acres of farm and pasture land. The Templetons moved into Haxtun in 1922, following the death of their son Dolf at the age of fifty. They sold the ranch in sections over the next few years. Albertine died in 1934 at the age of eighty-four. David died in 1936 at the age of ninety.

The cattle industry flourished for two decades before homesteaders gradually consumed the open range, putting up fences and breaking the sod. The cattlemen fought the intrusion, but once the government decided that cultivating the soil to grow crops would offer a better return than stock grazing, the cattle kings' arguments failed. The defeat of legislation to create a National Cattle Trail in 1885 sped the influx of farmers under the 1862 Homestead Act.

The distribution of government lands as outlined in the Articles of Confederation went through a number of adaptations before settlers reached northeast Colorado in the mid-1880s. The Land Ordinance of 1785 clarified the procedure for measuring boundaries by creating six townships within an unsettled territory and then dividing each township into thirty-six sections equal to one square mile, or 640 acres each. Policy required individuals to purchase entire sections of land for $1.00 per acre. The cost and labor needed to prepare the land for farming made it impossible for most citizens to purchase the land. The requirement shrank to a half section in 1800, but the price increased to $1.25 per acre, where it remained until 1854 when legislation instituted a scale based on "desirability of the lot." In 1860, Congress agreed on a homestead bill that provided federal land grants to western settlers, which President James Buchanan vetoed.

Two years later, on May 10, 1862, President Abraham Lincoln signed the Homestead Act establishing a process of acquiring land. Any citizen, or intended citizen, who had never borne arms against the United States could file an application to claim a one-quarter section or 160 acres of land; the homesteader was required to live on the land for five years and improve the land by constructing a twelve- by fourteen-foot dwelling and growing crops. After providing proof of residency and improvements and paying a small registration fee, the homesteader could file for his or her patent (deed of title). As an alternative, the homesteader could purchase the land for $1.25 per acre after a six-month residency and making trivial improvements.

The Coming of the Railroad

The Pacific Railroad Act, signed by President Abraham Lincoln on July 1, 1862, offered land grants to railroad companies in exchange for laying track in "designated" areas. The plan granted alternate sections of land along the line to the railroad with the government retaining ownership of the rest. The railroad companies, needing to sell land to cover the cost of building the rail line, advertised "bumper crops" grown in "fertile soil" on prairie land without stone, woods or "underbrush" and filled the ads with luring pictures. By 1869, the Transcontinental Railway wound its way across the frontier, bringing immigrants enticed by the ads.

The Union Pacific Railroad Company laid its first tracks in Colorado Territory, running from Nebraska to Julesburg in what was then Weld County, and completed its line from Sterling to Cheyenne, Wyoming, in 1869. Two years earlier, in 1867, a group of Denver merchants had incorporated the Denver Pacific Railroad and Telegraph Company with the goal of connecting Denver to Cheyenne. Construction began on October 4, 1869, in Cheyenne. The line, completed August 15, 1870, became the first major railroad to serve the Colorado Territory, stretching one hundred miles along a path that is now Colorado U.S. Highway 85.

In the meantime, the Kansas Pacific Railroad began laying tracks from Kansas City, Kansas, west toward Denver and through the southern portion of what are now Yuma and Washington Counties. The crews, working from both the east and west ends of the line, completed the track in August 1870. A few years later, the Colorado and Wyoming Railroad, a subsidiary of the Chicago, Burlington and Quincy (CB&Q) Railroad, constructed the "High Line" from Dewitt, Nebraska, to Cheyenne, passing through Holyoke, Paoli, Haxtun, Dailey, Fleming and Sterling before continuing on to the end of the line. A third line of tracks, laid by the Denver and Montana Railroad Company, entered Colorado at the Nebraska state line near Peetz in 1900.

In a memoir published in the *Greeley Tribune* in 1998, Jack H. Gillette wrote:

> *Homesteaders, lured by the promise of land promoters, would load all their worldly goods into emigrant cars and the railroad would take them wherever they wanted to go. Their car might have been sided off in a town or pushed onto a siding in the middle of nowhere. From there, the emigrants would move to their homestead. It's been said there were times when the emigrants would gaze over the prairie and quickly decide to have their car coupled to*

Trains became an important factor in the settling of the High Plains by bringing immigrants and their belongings to the area as towns sprang up beside railroad sidings. The railroad continued to provide a means for bringing supplies to the settlers and shipping products produced by farmers out, as well as providing transportation for travelers. Known as the "High Line," trains like this one, pictured with its crew, made daily stops at the Haxtun Depot. *Courtesy of Reon Chaney.*

> *the next train back to civilization. But there were others who stayed, built towns and developed good farms and ranches.*

Mary A. Fiedler, who came to Phillips County with her husband, Charles, in 1886, described the prairie as "sepia and silver" in the morning and "molten gold" at noonday, having sunsets with " long streamers of red and gold flung across that area of silver grass."

Another homesteader, as related in Conklin's *A Brief History of Logan County*, saw a less romanticized reality: "Trees will not live in the house yard, house owners can have no turf, no flowers, no fruit, no vegetables; the space around the dwellings in the towns is bare sand relieved only by infrequent mosses and weeds, the grass is gray upon the Plains."

Edna Mackey Call described a lone tree that grew a half mile west of Haxtun: "People would walk out there to sit in its shade."

The first patents recorded in Phillips County went to David J. Ritter for 80 acres and Curry B. Mason for 120 acres, both issued on August 30, 1886. The Mason homestead, located three and one-half miles south of Paoli below the Frenchman Creek, is now part of the Harold and Hazel Gall Trust. The Ritter land, seven and one-half miles south and three and one-half miles west of Paoli along Sandy Creek, is owned by Bamford Farms, LLC.

Bureau of Land Management (BLM) records list early patents spread intermittently over Phillips County, with ten issued in 1888 and another fourteen in 1889. The largest numbers issued in the county came in 1890, 1891, 1892, 1893, 1894 and 1895, when the BLM issued 378, 189, 92, 92, 136 and 111, respectively. The number of patents issued in the following years, between 1896 and 1930, gradually decreased, except in 1913, when the number rose to 63 before dropping again.

The homesteaders experienced a primitive and rugged life. Getting supplies meant slow travel by foot, on horseback or in a wagon pulled by horses. The treeless landscape provided no wood for construction or fuel, and a scarcity of water meant hauling barrels on wagons over miles of prairie. Homesteaders chased off marauding herds of Texas cattle that invaded the fields and pastures, as well as the occasional stray buffalo. A few Indians wandered about. Randy Overstreet recalled a story his grandmother told him about two Indian braves who visited the homestead of his great-grandparents, Washington and Emma Slay, near Haxtun. Emma and daughter Ruth were alone at the homestead when the two Indians burst through the door. Emma grabbed the young Ruth, holding her back as one of the Indians grabbed a pot of beans from the stove and left.

Randy Overstreet's grandmother Ruth Slay watches the photographer set up his camera to shoot photos of her parents' homestead north of Haxtun in the late 1890s. Ruth's father, Washington Slay, who served as a Phillips County commissioner, kept a daily diary describing life on the homestead from October 5, 1896, until September 1, 1899, ending each entry with commentary on the weather. *Courtesy of Randy Overstreet.*

Charles E. Erickson emigrated from Sweden to Iowa and, in 1885, traveled to Julesburg by train before walking the forty miles to his land southeast of Haxtun, where he made his first home in a dugout along the South Fork Creek. Charles B. Timberlake walked with Erickson. The dugout consisted of a depression carved into the hillside with a space for a doorway. Erickson lived in his dugout from the winter of 1885 until 1895, when he built a two-room sod house west of his creek home.

Construction of a sod house involved carving at least a half acre of buffalo grass sod into bricks and stacking them to the desired height with soil tamped between for mortar. These dwellings, although dreary and dark, provided warmth in winter and cool temperatures in summer. Shipped-in lumber provided doors, windows and ridgepoles. Some pioneers whitewashed the inside walls after plastering them with gypsum. Flour and sugar sacks attached to the ceiling held off dirt and insects. The sod roofs bloomed with native wildflowers in spring.

Elbert Coats, who moved to the Bryant community twelve miles south of Haxtun in 1887 at the age of eleven, explained how his grandfather, Wilson B. Coats, built the family's first home, a one-room dugout, by excavating a few feet in depth and then constructing sod walls around the hole to a height tall enough to allow for head room. He roofed it with rough boards covered with tarpaper and sod and installed a glazed sash in the window opening for light and ventilation. "The clay subsoil, when packed and dry, formed a floor surface almost as smooth as concrete," he wrote in *Those Were the Days*.

In *Our Pioneer Heritage*, published by the Fleming Historical Society, Ed Morris relates that his family came to Colorado in 1891 and lived for a time in a dugout that had dirt floors, two small windows and holes in the walls. At night, centipedes crawled along the roof's timber beams before falling off and landing on the bed. Sometimes the fall would kill them but not always. Snakes also visited, and one night as Ed's sister Kate sat reading with her back to a window, a rattlesnake slithered down her shoulder, across the floor and exited through one of the holes in the wall.

The following year, the family constructed a one-and-one-half story concrete house, gathering stones and mixing concrete in a coal-burning kiln located on a neighbor's farm. They brought in stone from the surrounding hills and dug down six to eight inches in the ground to find lime. It took two tons of coal costing five dollars per ton and hauled by horse and wagon from Sterling to operate the kiln. "We put six inches of kindling to start with, six inches of stone and six inches of coal on the top of the kiln. When we got it

The remains of a stone house built by pioneer John McDonald in the late 1880s still remains two and one-half miles east of Fleming and a half mile off Highway 6. McDonald, a stonemason, used rocks dug from the surrounding hills. The original house consisted of one room, but McDonald later added a second room. *Courtesy of Becky (Thomas) Jackson.*

filled, we set fire to the kindling and it burned for a week," Morris wrote. "It made some of the hottest lime I ever saw."

A one-room stone house built by John McDonald in the late 1880s still stands two and one half miles east of Fleming about one-quarter mile off Highway 6. McDonald, a stonemason who fought for the Union during the Civil War, migrated from Pennsylvania to Plum Creek, Nebraska, in 1872 and then came to Colorado by emigrant train with his wife, Sarah (Miller) McDonald, and their three children.

John McDonald raised draft horses from 1905 to 1909, served as a Logan County Commissioner and was among a group of men who traveled to Colorado's Front Range to look at designs for the Logan County Courthouse. Sarah McDonald baked bread, churned butter to sell to other homesteaders and grew peanuts in the summer to give as special treats to children at Christmas time. George Thomas, the couples' grandson, remembered his grandparents "sitting in rocking chairs in front of the corncob-burning stove, smoking their corncob pipes Appalachian style."

After 1909, a number of settlers ordered prefab homes from Sears, Roebuck and Company. Many of those homes, including the one Wayne and Doris Scott live in northwest of Haxtun, remain in use on area farms.

Charles Erickson cultivated his own land and helped other settlers locate in the area, working as a surveyor with Andrew Axelson. The two operated their land business, riding horseback between Julesburg and Haxtun. According to a 1935 *Harvest* article, Erickson and Axelson surveyed around 2,500 farms using a wagon with a rag tied to one of the wheel spokes and counting the revolutions of the wheel to measure the boundaries. Erickson also engaged in business with Charles Timberlake, gathering the bones of buffalo and other animals to sell for fertilizer. Erickson constructed a cement house in 1907 but, due to health concerns, retired from farming and sold the homestead to Evelyn Carnes in 1927. When Charles Erickson's grandson Wilbur Kipp married Evelyn Carnes's daughter Lois in 1948, the land came back into the family, where it remains.

Charles Erickson immigrated to America from Sweden at the age of twenty-two. He lived in Illinois and Iowa before coming to Colorado for his health. "Mr. Erickson boasted a colorful life of many experiences, having seen the prairie broken up by homesteaders and settlements built," wrote the *Harvest* following his death on June 2, 1935. "Through those early days of crop failures, blizzards and suffering from the lack of food, his experiences are typical of the western pioneer."

Charles Timberlake, who farmed and raised stock, served as superintendent of Phillips County Schools from 1889 to 1895 and as county clerk from 1895 until 1897. He was appointed receiver for the United States Land Office in Sterling on July 1, 1897, a position he held until April 30, 1914. The following year, Timberlake, a Republican, was elected to represent the sixty-fourth congressional district, serving until May 1933. He then worked in banking in Sterling until his death on May 30, 1941.

Born in Ostergotland, Sweden, in 1853, Andrew Axelson immigrated to America in 1869, settling first in Andover, Illinois, and later in Bertrand, Nebraska, before coming to Haxtun in 1885. "Mr. Axelson was one of the pioneers of Haxtun," wrote the *Harvest* after his sudden death on September 6, 1931. "He was a very public-spirited man and always interested in the improvement and building of the community. No question concerning the progress or betterment of Haxtun and the community escaped his attention, whether material, social or spiritual." The *Harvest* went on to note that Axelson "was especially interested in crop development and devoted a great deal of time to a study of crops best adapted to the area's climate and soil."

Finding wood on the prairie for any purpose was difficult. In 1887, James L. Wood homesteaded a quarter section of land three miles east of Haxtun, where he built a one-room sod house for his wife, Mary, and their four children. One day, James Hamilton arrived at the Wood homestead from the southeast and asked if they could spare any lumber to build a coffin to bury his little girl who had died from diphtheria. James Wood helped him build the coffin, and Mary Wood provided some artificial flowers from her hat as a memorial gift. They buried the little girl in a cemetery seven miles south of Haxtun. Since there were no ministers or churches at the time, James Wood conducted the service. The Wood family raised cattle, and both James and Mary taught school to supplement their income. The cattle, which they drove north into Nebraska during dry years, grazed on the open range.

In 1888, O.W. Painter, editor of the *State Herald* wrote, "The recent rains have put a new aspect on the appearance of things. It has inconvenienced the people who live in loose sod houses and shakes somewhat, yet, in the main it will do an inestimable amount of good." So much rain fell in May 1888 that "soddies" became "precarious" places that leaked and caved in, causing Painter to proclaim, "The sod house days are about past."

While rains soaked the area at the end of the 1880s, the early 1890s brought drought. When the crops failed and the pasture grass stayed brown throughout entire summers, family after family loaded their belongings into covered wagons and left. On August 17, 1894, the *State Herald* reported that "the coming winter will be a trying one for the homesteaders that stay, as there is no feed or at least very little, and there are but a few that have succeeded in raising anything." Those who stayed found work elsewhere and did what they could to feed their families and stay on the land.

Women raised gardens and chickens, made noodles from the eggs and dried fruit for winter use. In spring, they gathered dandelion greens and pigweed. They milked cows by hand and separated the cream to make butter, cream cheese, ice cream or whipped cream. They fed any milk not consumed by the family to the animals or left it to sour to make cottage cheese and then used the whey as liquid in making bread.

They used all parts of animals at butchering. Beef tallow made soap for washing and beeswax for candles. They drained the blood from butchered hogs to make blood sausage and used the ears in making headcheese. They cleaned, cooked and pickled pigs feet; cooked, skinned, pickled and sliced the heart and tongue of both beef and swine for sandwiches; and rendered the lard and used it to cover chunks of meat stored in stone jars kept in a cool

John H. Olson homestead north of Haxtun in 1887. John Olson worked for the Burlington Railroad and helped build the Haxtun train depot. He later built a grain elevator in Haxtun that he operated until his death in 1906. In bad years, John walked to Greeley to find work. The family hauled water until John dug a well that he used for irrigation, an ice plant in winter and a swimming pool in summer. *Courtesy of Reon Chaney.*

dark place. They cured the hams and bacons in salt brine and cleaned the intestines to stuff with ground scraps of meat to make sausage.

James H. Grover recalled burning cow chips and corncobs for fuel: "Poking corncobs in the fire was a never-ending job because, although they made a hot fire, they burned quickly like paper."

Despite the hardships, some came to love the open space, endless blue sky, mostly pleasant climate and the people with whom they shared the High Plains. Edward Robinson, who came to Colorado from Iowa in 1907 and settled northeast of Haxtun, wrote the following to a newspaper in Iowa: "I still think we are living in the garden spot of the world. The town of Haxtun and the country around it has come to the front in less time than old Iowa. Take the people as a whole, they seem to be the happiest that I ever met. This you find as you go West. We have the best climate of any state in the union. There are crops of all kinds; good land is on the boom."

In a memoir written in 1913, John H. Olson's son Roy related that settlers traveled across fields to Julesburg to purchase supplies in 1886 although Sterling, to the west, was closer: "It was almost an impossibility to get over the sand hills, and there was no highway of any kind between the two places." He remembered wild horses roaming the area and the settlers trying, in many cases unsuccessfully, to capture these "fine specimens." They held church services in homes built of sod with dirt floors. He noted, "There being no butcher shops, everyone was compelled to kill their own beef or pork. Few of the pioneers, however, tasted fresh meat. They survived on side meat, potatoes and flour." He said many settlers left discouraged, but "some are still with us enjoying at this time the fruits of their early toil" and the "reward in seeing these once semiarid plains blossom like a modern Garden of Eden."

Chapter Three

POST OFFICES, COMMUNITIES, COMMERCE AND POLITICS

When Joe J. Warren drove his covered wagon across the prairie, he encountered a barren wilderness. Arriving at his destination, Warren drove the bows from the covered wagon into the ground to provide a temporary shelter for his wife and two children while he built a sod house. The Warrens made the trip from Garnet, Missouri, crossing into Colorado at Julesburg in 1886.

Talking to the *Harvest* in December 1939, Warren recalled standing on a ridge and shooting antelope where the town of Haxtun now sits. Large herds of antelope and a small herd of around sixty-five buffalo provided an abundance of meat, and a two-day hunt filled his wagon box with game that fed his family and many of the neighbors, garnering him the nickname "Antelope Joe."

Droves of wild horses roamed the area, and a man named "Wild Horse Jeff" drove the horses to exhaustion so he could capture them. "This character was mysteriously shot and killed," said Warren as he related the struggles endured by pioneers moving into the area over the next two years, creating wagon grooves in the land between Julesburg and Haxtun.

Warren credited Ben Raymond with opening the first store a short distance from Haxtun and then moving it closer when news of a train siding reached him. "Opening a store added greatly to the convenience of those living in the community," said Warren, who later moved to Pinedale, Wyoming.

Andrew Hendrix, who arrived in 1886, also opened a general store. Hazel Ahnstedt, writing for the 1973 edition of *Those Were The Days,* claimed

Ben Raymond opened Haxtun's first general store a short distance from the original Haxtun town site around 1886 but moved it closer when he learned the railroad planned to put in a siding. *Courtesy of Reon Chaney.*

Andrew's wife, Lydia Bell Hendrix—later Mrs. L.H. Work—lived in the area for six months before she saw another woman. She operated the store with Andrew and, since no hotel operated at the time, offered room and board to newcomers. A fire destroyed the Hendrix store, which also housed the post office, in 1901.

The Ezekiel Scott family history notes that he and wife, Ruth, operated a general mercantile store in Haxtun during the 1880s. Though no record of the Scott store remains, BLM records show Ezekiel's sons Freemont and Washington received patents on land southwest of Haxtun in 1891 and 1893. The family moved to Nebraska in 1894, settling in the Scottsbluff/Gering area.

The Lincoln Land Company, a subsidiary of the Burlington and Missouri River Railroad, incorporated in the spring of 1880 to buy land and plat towns along the proposed railroad line running through Nebraska and other western states. The company laid out the northeastern Colorado towns of Amherst and Holyoke just before the tracks reached the Nebraska-Colorado state line on August 7, 1887, and Holyoke nine days later. Holyoke soon became a railroad division point with a five-stall brick roundhouse, a large depot and a restaurant for railroad passengers as an estimated ninety per day arrived from the east. On October 21, 1887, the *State Herald* wrote: "Little did we think when we came here a year and a half ago, finding nothing but buffalo grass and the cactus, that we would be blessed with two railroads and the beautiful city of Holyoke."

A week later, the newspaper began its campaign for "County Capital" of what was then Logan County. Despite the newspaper's effort to rally support, a December 20, 1887 election gave the county seat to Sterling. Holyoke, which incorporated on April 24, 1888, received its chance at county seat status when the legislature carved Phillips County from the southeastern corner of Logan County in 1889. The population of Phillips County reached 2,642 by 1890, dropped to a low point of 1,583 during the drought years and then rose again, reaching 5,499 by 1900.

The railroad originally surveyed a line from Holyoke southwest to Akron and based on that plan, the Lincoln Land Company laid out the town sites of Curtis, Burdett, Leslie, Rockland, Bryant, Emerson and Wakeman. The United States Postal Service established post offices at Wakeman on September 19, 1887, and at Bryant and Emerson on March 27, 1888. The Emerson Post Office consolidated with Holyoke on September 20, 1890. The Wakeman Post Office closed on May 15, 1897. The Bryant Post Office operated until March 31, 1916, when it moved to Burdette.

When the railroad surveyed an alternate route, Lincoln Land Company officials purchased homesteads from Kate Fletcher and Alice C. Strohm to establish the town of Haxtun seventeen miles west of Holyoke. Anselino B. Smith surveyed the "original Town of Haxtun" on June 2, 1888, the same date that officials of the Lincoln Land Company recorded the initial plat, which included the avenues of Utah, Logan, Colorado, Washington and Nebraska (no longer in existence) running north from the railroad tracks and the east–west streets of Raymond, Fletcher, Strohm and Chase. A warranty deed recorded on September 20, 1888, notes that Kate Fletcher received $1,176.75 for her homestead.

Alice Strohm, who served as Haxtun's first postmaster, petitioned the postmaster general on August 9, 1887, explaining that no post office served the region and settlers at present obtained their mail at Sterling, Julesburg or Yuma. "There are no bridges over the Platte between Julesburg and Sterling and an almost impassable range of sand hills stretch along the east bank," Strohm explained. She inserted "Haxtum" beside the name Raff, indicating that as her second choice since postal records already showed an office named Raff. The railroad spelled the town's name "Haxton" for a time, and the post office continued to spell it "Haxtum" until 1910, when a group of citizens petitioned the post office department to change the *m* to the appropriate *n*, as it appeared in the town's legal papers.

In his 1913 memoir, Roy Olson wrote that Washington Strohm, Alice Strohm's twenty-eight-year-old brother, occupied the first house in Haxtun and was the first person buried in the Haxtun Cemetery after he died from injuries allegedly sustained in a fight with a man named Malone at a Haxtun "saloon" on June 10, 1889.

As settlers continued to arrive, Haxtun's commerce grew. A May 12, 1899 *State Herald* news item reported that Haxtun had two general stores, a blacksmith shop, a creamery separator, a grain elevator and "more businesses are being transacted." In August, Hafen reported that "Haxtun as a trading point has been improving very materially during the past two years. It is located in the most prosperous section of the rain belt. The farmers are reasonably sure of a grain crop and most of them are interested in the stock industry."

People flowed into the area, and on April 6, 1900, the *State Herald* reported, "During the last week, seven carloads of emigrants [*sic*] and their goods have been unloaded in Haxtun. They were from Nebraska and it is thought about eighty new settlers altogether have settled along the Frenchman this spring."

The decision of the railroad not to lay track through Bryant halted the growth of that small village twelve miles south of Haxtun. A once thriving community of around fifty inhabitants with several businesses—including a grocery store, drugstore, blacksmith shop and a number of saloons—Bryant continued to decline, and in 1892, Manuel Anderson moved his store building and business from Bryant to Haxtun. The store carried general merchandise but later stocked furniture, farm implements and lumber. Anderson also dealt in cattle, hogs and wheat. The building, located at 229 South Colorado Avenue, later housed the Anderson Café. The Haxtun Community Federal Credit Union opened in 1938 and moved into Manuel Anderson's building where it remains today. Anderson also helped organize the Farmers State Bank in 1905. He moved to San Diego, California, in 1926, where he passed away on October 3, 1940. An obituary published October 9, 1940, in the *Harvest* related that Manuel Anderson helped many residents by extending credit.

Herbert Henry Dee, his wife, Amy, and two of their children came to Haxtun in 1903 and opened a store. The Dees, who recalled that there were no trees growing in Haxtun at that time, lived in the back part of the store. Herbert Dee, along with Dr. J.D. Cochran and C.H. Baker, purchased the Haxtun Drug Company from Smith and Chaney in 1919. A news item announcing the sale noted that H.H. Dee, president of the First National Bank, was also engaged in farming.

Birdseye view of Colorado Avenue in 1907 from the south end facing north. The Haxtun Hotel sits two doors north of the lumberyard. A white building to the north of the two-story building served as the Haxtun Post Office. A fire later damaged the backside of this two-story building, constructed in 1904. The Drake Mercantile building replaced this building in 1913. G.W. Gordon's Bank of Haxtun sat across Fletcher Street on the north side where the Haxtun Town Hall now sits. *Courtesy of Reon Chaney.*

Hazel Ahnstedt wrote that Haxtun "boasted" nineteen buildings by 1905, "including houses and barns." The December 20, 1907 edition of the *Haxtun E.L. Herald* advertised the Pioneer Land Company under the management of Andrew M. Axelson, the J.E. Yates Land Company and John. O. Anderson (dealer in dry goods, groceries, Queen's ware, fresh and salt meats, oysters and fish in season). Other advertisers included the Haxtun Drug Store (J.B. Johnson), the Bank of Haxtun, D.C. Warren Meat Shop, C.E. Johnson Stock Broker, Ed DeWolf (barber and photo man), George Smith Restaurant, B&M Land Company, Mrs. L.M. Hendrix Boot and Shoe Shop, R.E. Shearer Livery Feed and Sale Stable, E.H. Smith (manufacturer of "first class" cement blocks and posts) and M. Anderson (general merchandise, implements, lumber and coal, livestock and grain). A week later the newspaper added Haxtun's hardware man H.O. McNichols and Dr. J.E. Ford, physician and surgeon.

The original Town of Haxtun with two additions—South Haxtun platted by Elizabeth J. Decker on May 7, 1906, and the first portion of the Axelson addition platted by Andrew M. Axelson on December 18, 1907—incorporated on July 1, 1909.

The town's first officials met on July 20, 1909, to pass a dozen ordinances and appoint civil servants. Two years later, on June 2, 1911, the town council

Barbwire marks the south end of Colorado Avenue in this photo taken toward the north in 1908 or 1909. The gazebo at the corner of Colorado Avenue and Fletcher Street served as a stage for band concerts and other entertainment provided to farmers who came to town on Saturday to buy groceries and other supplies for the coming week. *Courtesy of Reon Chaney.*

granted J.A. Brooks of Haxtun Telephone Company the right to lay conduit underground and issued him a twenty-year license to operate a telephone system. Charges for service were not to exceed $2.50 per month for a one-party business phone; $2.00 per month for a two-party business phone or a one-party residential phone; and $1.50 per month for a two-party residential phone.

Telephone service actually began in 1903, when farmers strung lines on barbed wire fences and placed calls through a switchboard in the Wilbur Grove home north of Haxtun. According to Carol Scheel, granddaughter of J.A. Brooks, children walking home from school pulled the tumbleweeds off the fence to keep the reception clear. Around 1909, the switchboard moved to the home of Mrs. Hans Johnson on the corner of Washington Avenue and Raymond Street. The company moved to its present location on Fletcher Street in 1917. Brooks purchased the Dailey Telephone Company in 1917, combined it with Haxtun and began service seven days per week. Paoli Telephone Company, owned by Ira J. Taylor, became part of the system in 1935, shortly after J.A. Brooks turned the company over to his son, Ivan Brooks. Floyd Reyher purchased the company in 1949 and added the communities of Crook and Fleming to the system.

The Haxtun Hotel, located on the west side of the 200 Block of South Colorado Avenue, welcomed guests in 1911 as travelers arrived at the nearby Haxtun train depot. *Courtesy of Reon Chaney.*

A tragic fire on August 14, 1911, destroyed eleven buildings, claimed the life of twelve-year-old Elsie Kelsey and badly injured her father, L.L. Kelsey, and her sister Grace. A bucket brigade formed by citizens, several of whom narrowly escaped injury from falling walls, fought the blaze. The fire raged until it burned itself out, gutting one entire block on the east side of the 200 block of South Colorado Avenue. The fire started in a one-story wood building where the Kelseys operated a restaurant and lived in the rear.

In addition to the Kelsey restaurant, the fire destroyed the Bentson grocery store, Sherman's restaurant, the Haxtun Hardware Company, Bates Barber Shop, the Hendrix and McNichols Garage, an unoccupied building, Dr. Keesee's drugstore and Miss Blanch Campbell's millinery store. According to an August 18, 1911 *Holyoke Enterprise* story, the loss reached $25,000 with little insurance available for the business owners.

The fire sparked discussions on the need for a town-operated water system, which voters approved on February 18, 1913. The measure allowed the town to borrow $20,000 and levy taxes on property owners to pay for the

Workers piled debris pulled from the 1911 fire in front of G.W. Gordon's Bank of Haxtun. The bank sat on the northwest corner of the Colorado Avenue and Fletcher Street intersection. The white building on the southwest corner of that intersection held the Haxtun Post Office at this time. *Courtesy of Reon Chaney.*

Haxtun Municipal Power Plant, constructed in 1917. Men identified (left to right) as William Bruce, John Kirchofer, Edgar Jones and George Jones Jr. *Courtesy Town of Haxtun.*

principal and interest of the debt. The town created an electrical department in May 1917 and built a power plant that same year.

The Haxtun Fire Protection District organized on October 17, 1919, when the town council unanimously approved the expenditure of $250 for a chemical engine from Ajax Fire Engine Works and appointed Harvey O. McNichols chief and Nels Bentson assistant chief. Since no fire hall existed at that time, the town stored the engine in George Smith's saloon. Two years later, a group of eighteen men organized the Haxtun Volunteer Fire Department.

The town's first mortuary opened in 1919, and on March 20, the *Harvest* declared, "Contractor Nels Larson is putting up a fine bungalow for Harry Radford, the undertaker."

An ordinance creating a sewer system passed on June 21, 1920, but the town council put the system on hold after property owners protested. The *Harvest* reported, "A sanitary sewer for the entire village of Haxtun is apparently blocked at this writing, owing to the fact that the sentiment of the people of the town at large seems overwhelmingly against such an improvement." The council agreed to proceed with installing the sewer system for the "business part of the town," with the idea that the remainder of the town could be added later.

Fire was not the only danger to buildings during Haxtun's growing years. Due to the small creek that flowed through the northwest part of town toward the low areas, the north end of Colorado Avenue often turned into a small lake. Addie (Monteith) Monk, writing for *Those Were The Days*, recalled rafting with her brother Frank Monteith and friend Bill Green on a homemade raft. Ann Radford remembered riding down Colorado Avenue in a rowboat.

In March 1919, the *Harvest* advertisers included the Haxtun Tailoring Company, the Central Hotel and Houses, the O.D. Westergreen Store, the O.K. Barber Shop, the Farmers Grain and Trading Company, Haxtun Cabinet Works, the W.H. Albertshart Store, Anderson's (the Store of Correct Styles for Men) and the House and Land Company. There were also advertisements for automobile and farm machinery dealers, life and fire insurance, farm loans, land for sale and offers to look after nonresidents' property. A full-page ad stated, "100 men wanted at Haxtun, Phillips County, Colorado, in the corn, wheat and alfalfa belt; Land from $50 to $100 per acre, according to its distance from town and its improvements."

Opposite, bottom: House Land Company building, circa 1910–20, located on East Fletcher Street across from the Haxtun Telephone Company. *Courtesy of Reon Chaney.*

Built along the path of a creek, the north end of Colorado Avenue became a lake before the town of Haxtun created a drainage system during the 1930s. This photo taken in the early 1900s shows Andrew Axelson's farm in the background. *Courtesy Town of Haxtun.*

Dr. J.E. Rugg, Haxtun dentist, *right*, and John Milton Delander stand in front of their respective offices, circa 1916. The building, now stucco, still stands at the corner of Colorado Avenue and Raymond Street. *Courtesy of Scott Williams.*

The following week, the newspaper's advertisers included the Mack Mayberry Service Garage, which offered Texas gas and Texas oil along with automobile and "Fivver" accessories. Fivver was a slang term used for small, mass-produced cars such as the Ford Model T.

Professional cards included Dr. G.L. Cline, veterinary; Dr. J.D. Cochran, physician and surgeon; Dr. W. Keesee, physician and surgeon; Dr. G.E. Mallett, dental surgeon; Dr. E.S. Murray, physician and surgeon; Dr. J.H. McKnight, physician and surgeon; Dr. John E. Rugg, dentist; and Avery T. Searle, lawyer.

The landscape was also changing, as noted by an April 3, 1919 announcement that a large shipment of trees and shrubs arrived at the depot from the Empire Nursery in Sterling to "progressive citizens who are about to improve their places."

On April 10, 1919, the *Harvest* reported that the Spelts Grain Company elevator and other holdings passed into the ownership of the Farmers Cooperative Elevator Company, organized by some of the area's "most substantial farmers." The deal, instigated by the Farmers Union, included the manager's dwelling, six acres of land and the elevator for the "consideration of $12,500."

A Case combine parked behind the old Farmers Cooperative Elevator, circa 1920. The Case Company began building combines, first pulled by horses, around 1900. *Courtesy of Reon Chaney.*

Dr. James "Jim" H. McKnight showed his faith in the community in October 1919 by opening a hospital. The plan included moving the McKnights' residence to a new location and constructing an addition for the hospital. "The entire house will be finished in the most modern manner and conveniences of water, light and built in conveniences will be features of the home," noted the *Harvest*. "There will be a commodious basement and sleeping porches, bath and other of the things that the town dwellers of today regard as necessities to comfort." Dr. McKnight moved his practice to Sterling in 1936.

Drake Mercantile Company owners Dudley and Ed Finch and Ed Intermill constructed the two-story brick building located on the southwest corner of Colorado Avenue and Fletcher Street in 1913. The building housed the Farmers State Bank, a department store, a photography shop and a grocery store. The Haxtun Community Hospital, operated by registered nurses Formosa Newman of Knoxville, Tennessee, and Esther Jensen of Ord, Nebraska, opened on the second floor of the Drake Mercantile building on March 1, 1938. The women hoped to "make the hospital up to date in every respect," wrote the *Harvest* on February 23, 1938. They expected to use at least eight of the fourteen available rooms and to include a modern surgery department, with hospitalization available for "treatment of all cases, both surgical and medical."

Charles "Charlie" J. and Henrietta Elizabeth "Lizzie" (Warren) Johnson constructed the Shirley Hotel, a "handsome brick building" on the southwest

The Farmers State Bank, where robber William Thompson shot and killed cashier John Brunke on February 25, 1915, was located in the Drake Mercantile building that still stands at the corner of Colorado Avenue and Fletcher Street. The small building across the street to the north housed the Bank of Haxtun owned by G.W. Gordon. Circa 1916. *Courtesy of Reon Chaney.*

corner of Colorado Avenue and Strohm Street in 1921. Lizzie served as hotelier, and Charlie ran the Johnson Meat Company, which supplied the "choicest" of meats to the hotel's dinning room. The building also housed a refrigeration plant that produced block ice.

The hotel's lobby, which served as a gathering place for traveling salesmen, included a cigar counter, where "men lingered to debate the flavor and aroma of their favorite brands," wrote Velma Baylor in the 1993 *Phillips County History*. "Cribbage was a favorite game in the lobby," but rumor spoke of a poker room concealed in the basement.

The Johnsons later lost their holdings in the Shirley, but Charlie continued to operate his meat market while Lizzie went to beauty school. In October 1925, the *Harvest* reported that Charles Olson purchased the Shirley Hotel and took charge of its operation. The Johnson Meat Market and ice plant remained in the building until Charlie Johnson closed it in November 1935. The *Harvest* called Charlie "one of Haxtun's most highly respected business men."

A group of investors—A.J. Anderson, P.A. Peterson, E.G. Eaton, C.J. Latta, H.H. Dee and J.M. Delander—constructed the building located on the southeast corner of Colorado Avenue and Fletcher Street in 1918 to house the First National Bank of Haxtun. The building went on the tax rolls in 1919. Glen Jones, who served as town clerk from 1956 to 1978, recalled the bank's clock chiming at noon to mark the end of World War I. The excitement

Charlie and Lizzie Johnson constructed the Shirley Hotel on the southwest corner of Colorado Avenue and Strohm Street in 1920-21. The "handsome" brick building, considered "state of the art" at that time, featured fine dining with choice cuts of meat from Charlie's meat market that he also operated in the building. *Courtesy Town of Haxtun.*

Haxtun Town Hall occupies the building constructed in 1918 to house the First National Bank of Haxtun. The building went on the tax rolls in 1919. The First National Bank closed in 1932 for lack of funds and never reopened. The town of Haxtun purchased the building for back taxes in 1939. The interior looks much the same as it did when the bank operated, with the teller windows, marble counter top and baseboards, as well as the original leaded glass and hand-laid tile flooring. *Author photo.*

and celebration continued into the night, with several "outhouses" hauled into town and set afire in the middle of Colorado Avenue as the crowd cheered. Cars drove up and down the "dirt" street, and the fire department pulled out the handcart used to pump water in case any fires got out of control.

Alice (Tayor) Bamford, writing for *Those Were the Days*, recalled the "solemn" day in 1932 during the Depression, when the First National Bank closed due to lack of funds. The town of Haxtun purchased the building for back taxes in June 1939 to use as town hall. The clock stopped running when the bank closed, and the chimes stopped sounding due to needing repairs. When the town took ownership of the building, officials restarted the clock but determined repairing the chimes would be too costly.

SATURDAY NIGHT SOCIALIZING AND SHOPPING

Saturday nights resembled a celebration, "like big circus day," reported the *Harvest* on April 1, 1920, "when the normal population of Haxtun is trebled." Entire families came to town on Saturdays to purchase groceries and socialize. They left their orders with the grocery store clerks and then spent the evening visiting with friends and neighbors or attending a movie at the Rialto Theater. Those wanting a parking place arrived early. When the time arrived to go home, shoppers returned to the store to pick up their orders.

In May 1929, Haxtun merchants organized a Commercial Club, and that July, J.C. Penny Company opened in Haxtun after purchasing a store owned by J.B. Byars. The following year, a time when six other grocery stores operated in Haxtun, Mr. and Mrs. L.L. Baker of Atwood opened Baker's Red and White Grocery in the Smith-Chaney building on the northeast corner of Fletcher Street and Colorado Avenue. The Bakers displayed bushel baskets of fresh fruit along the side of the store and most canned goods came in gallon containers. The Bakers often traded groceries for eggs, which brought about fifty cents a dozen at that time.

John Spanger, who delivered groceries in a green van with the name of the store printed on the side, purchased the City Grocery and Market,

Opposite, bottom: When owners of the Haxtun Community Bank demolished the Smith-Chaney building in 1974 to make room for a new bank building, Reon Chaney watched with his uncle and later, went through the rubble to find the building's header. He placed it on his farm north of Haxtun as a memorial to his ancestor. *Author photo.*

The Smith-Chaney building, fourth from the left, was constructed in the early 1900s by partners Mr. Smith and Mr. Chaney, who ran the Haxtun Drug Store. They sold the drugstore to Herbert Dee, Dr. J.D. Cochran and C.H. Baker in 1919. The second story hosted movies and other social events. The photographer stood at what was the north end of town and aimed the camera southeast. Points West Community Bank now sits on this corner. *Courtesy of Reon Chaney.*

located in the Drake Mercantile building, in 1938 from B.B. Williams. The store opened early in the morning and closed at six o'clock in the evening Monday through Friday but remained open until "the last man left the pool hall" on Saturday nights.

Following the closing of the W. Clyde Moore men's store in 1941, Baker's Red and White moved into a building on the west side of Colorado Avenue, two doors north of town hall, and changed to self-service, where the customers gathered the groceries and checked out at the cash register.

The Bakers affiliated with Associated Grocers of Colorado, Inc. in 1953 and changed the store's name to Baker's Foodliner. L.L. Baker sold the store to his sons Raymond and Veylerd and daughter Elaine (Baker) Starr in 1955. The new owners purchased a building on the east side of Colorado Avenue and moved the store there in 1962. They sold the store in February 1978 to Bill and JoAnn Harris, who had purchased the A&F Grocery & Market from Frank and Arlene Baumgartner the previous November. The couple combined the two stores, renamed them Harris Grocery and Market and operated out of the Baker building. The merger brought the number of grocery stores down to two, with Haxtun Supers housed in the cement block building located on Logan Avenue. The Harris family ran the store until June 1989, when they sold their inventory to Haxtun Supers owner Perk O'Dell. Haxtun Supers built a new store on Highway 6 in June 1997.

In 1939, Hazel Ahnstedt recorded the population of Haxtun as 1,020 and wrote that the town covered an area of 103 square blocks. She noted, "The majority of residents in the community are descendants of early western pioneers."

AUTOMOBILES, DEPRESSION AND HIGHWAYS

After 1920, most Saturday night shoppers drove to town in automobiles, which slowly replaced the horse and wagon. In April 1920, the Phillips County Clerk's office licensed 1,430 motor-powered machines of seventy-one different makes, and in 1921, the *Harvest* reported "2,000 licenses will be issued this year in a county where motor vehicles were introduced in 1908—nearly every family has a car."

Automobiles did not necessarily mean things were easier. Earl Scott, writing about mail delivery in a Model T Ford, explained that hardly a day went by without a flat tire, and since the Model T came with "dismountable"

Autos parked in the 200 Block of South Colorado Avenue in 1910. John Milton Delander owned the car parked fourth from the left. Fire later damaged the backside of the building on the right, constructed in 1904. The two-story brick Drake Mercantile building, which still stands on the southwest corner of Colorado Avenue and Fletcher Street, replaced it in 1913. *Courtesy of Scott Williams.*

rims, the driver needed to take the tire off, patch the tube and put it back on the wheel before pumping it up with a hand pump.

Once automobiles improved, making trips across the country easier, the need for better roads increased. One early byway, a dirt road running along the railroad track and marked by arrows painted on scrap lumber or fence posts, passed through Phillips and Logan Counties on its way to Denver. Originally called the OLD (Omaha-Lincoln-Denver) Highway and later the DLD (Detroit-Lincoln-Denver) Highway, area merchants gathered at Sterling in 1924 to push for making the DLD part of the Harding Memorial coast-to-coast highway. "The proposed highway will be one of the best in the United States and has already been paved for hundreds of miles in many of the eastern states," wrote the *Harvest.*

Colorado Department of Transportation's (CDOT) *Highways to the Sky* publication claimed that northeastern Colorado's farming towns welcomed highway construction as economic development: "As more miles of highway became paved and attracted more cars and trucks, there was a need for garages to sell them, mechanics to repair the vehicles, filling stations to provide gas and hotels and cafes where travelers could stop for the night or eat meals."

George Jones Sr. prepares to take a spin in his 1913 Buick. In 1920, the Phillips County Clerk's Office licensed 1,430 motor-power machines of seventy-one different makes, and by the following year, nearly every Phillips County family owned a vehicle. *Courtesy of Reon Chaney.*

A check of traffic on the road showed that 75,000 cars passed through Haxtun in 1923, and newspaper advertisements in the 1920s substantiate the development of automobile-related businesses. However, roads and automobiles also took business away. "Most rural Coloradoans saw the car as a way out rather than a medium bringing in tourists dollars," wrote the CDOT. "Similar to other agricultural regions nationwide, residents of northeastern Colorado wanted better roads to take their products to market and to shop in the state's cities."

The National Recovery Administration (NRA) created by President Franklin Roosevelt's Depression-era "New Deal" in 1933 provided relief funds for a number of improvement projects, including the construction of U.S. Highway 6, which replaced the DLD Highway. When the CDOT appropriated $130,000 in funding to grade, surface and oil Highway 6 between Fleming and Holyoke, the *Harvest* reported that the Phillips County Commissioners would negotiate with property owners to obtain the right-of-way for the new highway, a "huge construction project" that was part of a relief measure for the unemployed. The Haxtun to Paoli portion of the road utilized 160 farm horses and one hundred men at a cost of around $21,000.

Farmers brought hayracks, which they turned on their sides in a semicircle and used as a windbreak to shelter the large number of horses during idle time. They moved the hayracks from one location to the next as the work progressed, eliminating the need to drive the teams from the farm to the job each day. Later, the Haxtun Commercial Club formed a committee to search for stable room in vacant barns and machinery sheds around town.

In September 1934, the *Harvest* reported that the CDOT expected to begin oiling Highway 6 through Phillips County from Fleming to Paoli, leaving the strip between Paoli and Holyoke, which was not included in the budget. Officials expected to budget for that portion the following year. The CDOT completed the oiling project through Phillips County to the Nebraska state line in November 1936.

In April 1936, a delegation from area towns, including Haxtun, Joes and Yuma met with the state highway advisory board seeking to promote Highway 59, established in 1920 as "a major north and south route through Colorado." The state paved the highway, which extends north to Highway 138 near Sedgwick and south to U.S Highway 40 at Kit Carson, two years later.

The NRA provided relief funds for a number of Haxtun's improvement projects, including the paving of Colorado Avenue from Strohm Street to Highway 6. The project started in August 1933 and included drainage on Strohm and Fletcher Streets, the widening of the sidewalks and the installation of ornamental lights along both sides of Colorado Avenue to First Street. The town added a curb and guttering for three blocks of Colorado Avenue's business district from the Burlington depot to the Shirley Hotel the following year, with labor again provided by relief workers.

In February 1934, Leslie E. Taylor, publisher of the *Harvest*, became administrator of the Civil Works Administration (CWA) and certifying officer of the Federal Relief Committee. He immediately reorganized the office and requested more relief funds to cover the growing number of applications for help. In May 1934, Taylor outlined three proposed relief projects, including the construction of the three-foot high, two-foot thick rock wall that surrounds the Haxtun Park; cleaning out the storm sewers; and repairing, manufacturing and replacing water meters. The park project included constructing several feet of sidewalk and planting grass between the curb and the rock wall. "The park at Haxtun is one of the finest maintained by any community in the state and has been the scene of many picnics during the summer," wrote the *Harvest* in September 1937.

The relief workers received orders for groceries, rent, utilities, fuel and other necessities, with each worker allotted a certain number of workdays and commodity orders. The businesses filling the orders received reimbursement from state relief funds. Wilbur Kipp said workers went out and picked up rocks in the country, hauled them into town and dumped them south of the Haxtun American Legion building before loading them into wheelbarrows and wheeling them to the park. The process extended the amount of time the workers put in.

Relief funds continued into 1935, when the town received $7,183 from the Works Progress Administration (WPA) to construct a swimming pool, install lights at the park and hire a part-time librarian. The town paid $1,812 toward the projects, which promised to employ a large number of men.

The town began its WPA swimming pool project in 1936 but placed it on hold while it focused on other infrastructure, including the WPA-funded replacement of water mains. Work on the town's swimming pool project, which included sidewalks surrounding the pool and dressing rooms, resumed in May 1937 with the aid of fifteen WPA workers. The town filled the pool the third week of June 1937.

WPA workers constructed the curb and gutter along both sides of Highway 59 in December 1938, utilizing a forty-man crew. The project, with the cost fixed at $3,045 by the WPA, included regrading the street, installing drains and replacing sidewalks. All WPA projects in Phillips County terminated on June 30, 1941, when the *Harvest* predicted a reduction in WPA workers due to men finding private employment.

Automobiles were not the only mode of transportation making life easier for the pioneers. In 1920, the *Harvest* reported, "Haxtun Aero Club is First One in State: Enterprising Haxtun Men Scoop Colorado on Flying Machine Company." The "progressive" officials of the Haxtun Aero Club—general manager L.C. Hartman, president Leonard Sharpe and secretary-treasurer W.J. Miles—constructed a hangar on a plot of land east of town. "The name is not based on fancy," wrote the *Harvest*. "Haxtun has an established firm with airplanes in stock, doing commercial work and teaching the business to others."

Descendants of the Haxtun Aero Club pilots continued the flying tradition, and in 1964, brothers Marlow and Keith Sharpe negotiated the purchase of twelve acres of ground one mile east and one mile south of Haxtun at a cost of $200 per acre from Gade Harms for the construction of an airport. The first runway operated without lights, requiring the pilot to improvise by flying over to notify other pilots who then parked their vehicles along the runway and used their cars' flashing lights to guide the pilot's landing.

Veylerd Baker became a certified flight instructor in 1975 and taught fifteen students who earned pilot certification, including two women—Fay McGuire (Ab Fleming's daughter) and Naida Bamford. The runway provided emergency services as well. Baker and Lloyd Ensminger flew in emergency blood for patients at Haxtun Hospital, while other pilots, including Greg Bamford and Damon Koch, flew residents to visit ill relatives confined in hospitals around the state.

Singer/songwriter John Denver landed at the Haxtun Airport in 1977. A small gathering of family and friends met his airplane, a Cessna 210, when it landed at 9:30 a.m. on July 2. "Denver, whose real-life name is Deutschendorf, left quickly with family members to nearby farmland where the winter-wheat harvest was in full swing," wrote the *Harvest*, which went on to relate that Denver's relatives from Kansas came to the area each summer to harvest the fields.

News of Denver's arrival spread quickly, and by early afternoon, the Tip Top Motel received ten calls. "It got to be a joke after awhile," said motel owner Jim Ellis. "The girls would call asking for him, and I just told them he couldn't talk at the moment because of all the noise and the crowd outside." The visit ended at 4:15 p.m., when the country-folk singer flew away, his take off less than effortless, according to the *Harvest*: "As bystanders watched, Denver, who had some trouble getting the engine started, piloted the plane away."

Not all of the flights out of Haxtun ended well. Harold Jessen and Harold Chaney left the Haxtun Airport on May 2, 1949, intending to land in Colorado Springs but died when the plane encountered a storm and crashed.

PAOLI EVOLVED BELATEDLY INTO A TOWN

Located nine miles east of Haxtun, the town of Paoli evolved belatedly despite the establishment of both a post office and school in June 1888. The school recorded twenty-two students that first year. The post office remained open until February 11, 1890, when the postal service closed it, routing the mail to Holyoke.

Until 1908, when the CB&Q Railroad constructed a wooden shed with stockyards and sat a boxcar along the railroad tracks to use as a depot, all that marked the Paoli siding was a painted sign placed along the track. Passengers wanting to board the train waved it to a stop.

Herbert Henry Dee and Oscar W. Lohn Sr. purchased 210 acres of land and requested a survey and platting of the original Town of Paoli on November 1, 1909, but the town waited another twenty years to incorporate.

The original plat included the east–west streets of Dee and Chaney with Lohn and Grant Avenues running north to south.

Two narratives claim the naming of Paoli. One, possibly someone's attempt at humor and recorded by J. Frank Dawson in *Colorado Place Names*, is that a Swedish railroad worker named "Ole" became angry while laying track near the town site and, upon quitting his job, shouted at the timekeeper, "Pay Ole." Thus the name Paoli evolved.

A second story credits a CB&Q Railroad engineer from Paoli, Pennsylvania, with naming the site after his hometown, which was named after Pasquale Paoli, a general and patriot from the European Island of Corsica. Pasquale Paoli's attempts to liberate Corsica from the French ultimately failed and resulted in his exile to London, where he died in 1807.

By March 9, 1910, when the postal service reopened its post office, Paoli claimed a blacksmith, billiard hall, restaurant, lumberyard, hotel (offering sleeping rooms and meals) and a grain business that operated in a small building off a loading dock near the railroad siding. Farmers poured their grain into burlap bags and loaded them onto railroad cars for shipment.

Phil Peters and Claud Lay constructed Paoli's first building on the west side of the railroad tracks in 1906. Phil and his wife, Lavina, operated a general store in the building, stocking groceries on the south side and clothing and other supplies on the north side, while the family lived in the rear. The post office occupied the northwest corner of the store. A wooden hitching post ran nearly sixty feet across the front of the building's exterior.

Ernest Cheramy constructed Paoli's second building, a pool hall with two tables and a number of slot machines, south of the Peters' store. These were the first slot machines seen by many in the community. Roy Dinsmore traded his homestead to the Peters for their store in 1918 only for it to burn down in 1920. Tom Guernsey then erected a large dance hall at that location, often holding four dances per week with music provided by traveling musicians. In the mid-1920s, the dance hall closed, and Ed Kurner purchased the building to open a grocery store. Other businesses that opened during the early 1900s included a lumberyard that later sold to the Foster Lumber Company, a drugstore built by Charles Gale and Jess Humphrey's grocery store.

After closing his dance hall, Tom Guernsey dug a well, built a barn and ran a livery stable where farmers watered their livestock when they hauled grain to town. Guernsey's well and windmill soon replaced other wells dug around town, and he supplied water to the residents of Paoli for many years. He used running gears to load galvanized tanks filled with water onto a wagon pulled by horses. Residents paid him fifty cents to fill their cisterns.

Charles Gale and E.E. Woods operated this drugstore in Paoli in the early 1900s. The interior included an ice cream counter and several tables. *Courtesy of Reon Chaney.*

Barefoot kids followed close behind the wagon during summer hoping that water splashing out of the tanks might run down their legs.

Harry Johnson opened a second pool hall in 1912 but soon traded it to brothers Charlie and Claud Horman for a "one-cylinder Hart-Parr" tractor that he used to break sod and plant wheat on his farm two miles north of town. The pool hall, which changed owners over the years, remained open until 1989.

In July 1919, fire consumed the boxcar that served as Paoli's depot along with three freight boxcars. The loss included eighty dollars in currency and all of the books and records kept in the depot. According to the *Harvest*, the operator who discovered the fire managed to roll a barrel of gasoline out of the depot, likely preventing an explosion and the loss of nearby buildings. The boxcar, which sat on a foundation, served as ticket office, freight and express office and telegraph station. The *Harvest* concluded, "The loss of the old boxcar depot likely will not be much regretted by the people of Paoli. While it is regretted that its removal should have occasioned so much loss, it also is likely that it will result in a suitable depot being built at this point, which is located in the heart of one of the best grain growing districts in the state."

A few weeks later, the *Harvest* reported that the Public Utilities Company ordered the construction of a new depot "of the regulation type prescribed for depots of that class."

The year 1919 proved prosperous for Paoli and the surrounding farms, according to the *Harvest*: "This thriving little town to the east of Haxtun is growing and prospering in a way that is gratifying to those who have pinned their faith to it through all stages of its development. So rapidly has the town grown and so active is business that it is hard to realize that less than five years ago this was nothing more than a whistling station for trains."

By 1925, four elevators with capacity to hold ninety thousand bushes of grain operated in Paoli, with over five hundred railroad cars of grain shipped annually. Outbound freight included corn, wheat, cream and eggs, while incoming freight consisted of livestock feed, coal and lumber.

Nineteen Paoli businesses advertised in the *Enterprise* in the mid-1920s. The town boasted an elementary school and a high school with seventeen students and a boys' basketball team. Residents could attend the Presbyterian or the Methodist church, and hundreds of people came to celebrate at Paoli's Fourth of July event, which included a rodeo and baseball games.

Although a fire destroyed the drugstore owned and operated by Charles Gale and Oscar Lohn, the men quickly constructed a new cement block building in its place, and on March 4, 1926, Paoli's business owners chartered the Paoli Chamber of Commerce, with the annual membership fee set at one dollar. The chamber immediately organized a Paoli ball team and agreed to furnish ten new suits without cost to the players and to divide any profits among the players who stayed with the team throughout the season. Chamber members oversaw alleys, repaired and constructed roads and culverts and, in 1929, organized a fire department, electing W.C. Seeman as chief and Ed Koerner assistant chief.

In August that year, the chamber hosted Paoli's first Harvest Jubilee and Rodeo, which the *Harvest* deemed a "great success." The day included a ball game between the Haxtun Harvesters and the Paoli team.

The Paoli Town Council recorded its first meeting on September 22, 1930, with E.P. Koener, C.F. Kruse, O.W. Lohn, J.A. Miles, V.E. Miller, E. Nelson and W.C. Seeman attending. Once Koerner took the oath of office as Paoli's first mayor, he nominated W.S. Johnson as town clerk, J.L. Porter as town marshal, Alber P. Smith as police magistrate and T.E. Munson of Sterling as town attorney. The council agreed to pay Marshal Porter two dollars a year plus "whatever fees there might be."

Trustees took care of the town's streets "at such wages as could be agreed upon at the time of doing the work and to do such work only as directed."

They resolved to meet at the American Legion Hall for "consideration to the Legion of $2 per meeting, with Legion providing lights and heat."

On January 3, 1931, Ira J. Taylor, L.J. Cheramy, G. Guernsey and Walter Biesemeier filed a case in the Phillips County District Court "attacking the incorporation of the Town of Paoli." The suit charged that the July 17, 1930 petition calling for incorporation was illegal because twenty-eight of the thirty-seven electors who signed it were not "bona fide residents." They accused Oscar W. Lohn Sr. of perpetrating a "fraudulent scheme" by signing contracts on property with a "fictitious purchase price" with full knowledge that the contract would not be completed "in order to give color of compliance with statutory provisions." It further claimed that since the petition was invalid, County Treasurer T.H. Hargreaves should be "enjoined and restrained" from collecting any tax levy. The court ultimately ruled that the incorporation was "regular in every way."

In 1933, Ira J. Taylor and A.R. Butler purchased controlling interest in the Paoli State Bank, and a few months later, robbers pried open a screen and window, entered the bank and attempted to burn through the vault with an acetylene torch. The torch failed to open the heavy "manganese safe" that contained the bank's main cash supply but succeeded in opening a smaller safe that held a small amount of money. A witness reported that he saw three men hanging out near the bank earlier but did not notice where they went.

In 1934, the Paoli town council held discussions with the CDOT regarding the "menace of flood waters" and wrote to the CB&Q Railroad about its bridge "hindering the natural flow of water" during flood season. Flooding became a major concern in August 1944, when a warning went out to residents that rain water from the Fleming-Dailey area to the west would soon reach Paoli. When the water arrived, it banked up against the highway bridge and flowed into town, flooding basements and residential dwellings. The water reached over the running boards of trucks driving down Highway 6, reported the *Harvest.* Potable water became a problem from the flooding as well: "Many other outdoor caves and all the wells were filled with water and was a problem to secure drinking water in the town." Water came from a creek south of Haxtun that ended near Paoli and emptied in the flats north of the railroad track.

On April 2, 1945, the council began discussions on purchasing a well and enough ground from Tom Guernsey to install a water system. Discussion on a water system continued into 1951 and 1952, and in October 1953, the council agreed to lay a water pipe from the town well.

In 1954, the council approved the purchase of the building known as the "bank building" for $700 to use as a town hall. The town removed the bricks from the exterior of the building and replaced them with sheet siding in August 1976. Remodeling in the early 1990s added a dining room, kitchen with a stove and refrigerator and a bathroom to the building, which continues to serve as a town hall and community center.

The town installed an up-to-date water system in 1977 and, the following February, signed a contract with co-contractors Louis Harman and Rick Ensminger to lay clay sewer pipe.

The Paoli Post office closed for the second time in 2012, this time possibly for good, but the community remains robust with pride. A hand-painted sign on the east edge of town speaks to how Paoli's citizens feel. It reads: "Please do not drive like hell through our town. It is Heaven to us." Marilyn Miller, whose property the sign sits on, served as Paoli's Postmaster from December 11, 1971, until she retired on July 1, 2012. She continues to serve as town clerk, a job she took on January 13, 1976.

Miller's town council meeting minutes often show the personal nature of small-town politics. She once wrote that Trustee Mo Smith arrived late for a meeting because "he had to finish a pool game with his wife." Another time she made note that Melinda Groshans (her daughter) and Sharon Thompson rented the town hall for the afternoon and paid the ten-dollar rental charge. "These girls also left cake and spiced cider for each board member."

In January 1985, the town set up a $500 emergency fund for Ed Neiman to help repair the damage his property sustained in a fire and agreed to pay a $120 hospital bill for Roger Warner, who cut his hand putting up Christmas decorations at town hall. In April 1985, the council appointed Jim McBee "official trash dumpster guard," with Trustee Linda Smith filling in when "Jim isn't available." The guard was needed to keep people from filling the town's dumpster with beer bottles.

Paoli mayor Virgil Harms may hold the record for the "longest-tenured" mayor in Colorado history, speculated *Denver Post* reporter Monte Whaley in 2011. The council appointed Harms mayor pro tem on August 24, 1959, to sign a liquor license for the pool hall since Mayor Oscar Lohn was not able to sign it. When Lohn died on November 3, 1961, Harms officially became mayor.

Harms grew up six miles north of Paoli then left for a time in the mid-1940s to serve in the army. The year he returned, 1947, Paoli's population stood at eighty and the business community included three grocery stores, a bank, hardware store, barbershop and pool hall. In the 1950s, as cars and roads improved, people moved away, and those who stayed began driving distances to shop. The 2010 census reported Paoli's population at thirty-four,

The Town of Paoli purchased the "bank building" in 1954 for $700 to use as town hall. In 1976, it replaced the brick exterior with siding and later added a dinning room, kitchen and stove. The building also serves as a community center for the town. *Author photo.*

but Marilyn Miller said she counted fifty-one until recently when five people moved away.

Mayor Harms, who at eighty-four continues to farm and square dance with his wife, Eloise, told Whaley that Paoli is "not exactly prosperous," but the population remains stable and the "downtown grain elevator is going strong" with eight employees. Perhaps fittingly, Mayor Harms lives on a street named Harms Way.

DAILEY ABUNDANT WITH HISTORY

Little remains in Dailey except skeletons of grain elevators, a few homes and a pioneer history that began in June 1914 when the CB&Q Railroad placed a siding six miles west of Haxtun. At that time, "a passenger on the High Line railroad looking from the window of his coach at the spot where the little town of Dailey now stands would have seen nothing on the south but a wide prairie with a few scattered farm houses in the distance," wrote Mabel Frank in a 1919 *Harvest* article.

The railroad placed the siding after area farmers requested a switch that would shorten the distance needed to haul grain for shipping. Ross Frank, son of Guy and Mabel Frank, speculated that a member of the train's switching crew named the siding Dailey after his surname.

Soon after the installation of the siding, the farmers organized the Farmers' Grain and Trading Company at Haxtun and built a scale office at Dailey. That fall, the Twidale Elevator Company constructed an elevator and quickly sold out to the Plains Milling and Mercantile Company of Haxtun. That business sold within a few days to the Longmont Farmers' Elevator, which became the Dailey Trading Company. The new owners constructed a general store and contacted Guy and Mabel Frank of Kearney, Nebraska, asking them to manage it. The couple, making the trip by horse and wagon, arrived in time to open the store in March 1915. The Franks purchased the store from the Dailey Trading Company in the spring of 1918 and renamed it the Dailey Cash Store. Guy Frank died from a self-inflected gunshot wound in 1923.

Mabel Frank, who ran the store for forty-seven years, later married Norton Markham. After his mother's death in 1962, Ross Frank closed the store but

The Dailey Cash Store, operated by Mabel Frank-Markham from 1915 to 1962, carried canned goods on the left side and dry goods on the right. A broom rack and bananas hung from the ceiling, while horse collars, scoop shovels, wash boilers and tubs, cream cans and milk buckets sat near the back wall. The building also housed the Dailey Post Office in the right rear corner. *Courtesy of Ross Frank.*

Dailey School's boys' basketball team beat La Junta to win the Logan County Tournament in 1938, then lost to Englewood in the State Tournament. Players included, *back row, left to right*: Cecil Mock, Wayne Hinde, Melvin Spanger, Bud Grauberger, Glen Kelley and Warren Heckman; *front row, left to right*: manager Kenneth Hurst, Les Anderson, Buell Mock, Ross Frank, Art Wheeler and coach C.M. Bertagnolli. *Courtesy of Ross Frank.*

continued to maintain the building. He donated the building to the Logan County Historical Society and moved it to the Overland Trail Museum Park in Sterling in 1992.

In 1915, country schoolhouses located near each farming family were numerous, wrote Ross Frank. "Several families lived on each square mile and most included four to six children. Since Dailey sat in the middle of a township, it seemed the ideal location to build a consolidated school to serve the area."

Once residents voted to consolidate, the men worked "untiringly to build a school the community could take pride in," wrote Mabel Frank. The resulting twelve-grade brick school completed in 1916 became the first consolidated school in Colorado and the first to use school buses, according to the Logan County Economic Development Corporation. Mabel Frank credited "Tom Clark with hauling yards and yards of gravel"

A memorial commemorates the Dailey School, established in 1916 as the first consolidated school in Colorado and the first to use buses. The school consolidated with Fleming in 1964. *Author photo.*

for the project and wrote that she baked "loaves and loaves of bread" to feed the construction crew. Principal T.E. Breezeley opened the school that first year with sixty students enrolled in grades one through twelve and four teachers—Miss Eva Ravenscroft, Miss Julia Mahler, Mrs. Florence Perrigo and Mrs. Charles Graves. Ernest Wheeler served as janitor, while B.L. Faris, W.L. Bamford and R.R. Fouts drove the "jitney" or school bus.

The addition of a gymnasium in 1926 provided a place for school plays, basketball games and community activities such as literary nights, box suppers, pie socials, farm organization meetings and political rallies. "The athletic teams at Dailey School were always competitive and sportsmanlike," wrote Ross Frank. "The Dailey girls' basketball team of 1926 put Dailey on the map when they defeated all local competition and went to the State Tournament."

In 1938, the boys' basketball team defeated Akron, Julesburg and Wray in District Tournament to earn a trip to the State Tournament. The team defeated La Junta, 47–29, in the first game but fell to Englewood, 34–20, in the second. The Dailey School consolidated into Fleming's Frenchman RE3 District in 1964.

The school's gym provided a place to serve lunch during the rabbit drives held across the area throughout the 1920s and 1930s. A January 15, 1925

Rabbit hunts, popular in the late 1920s and early 1930s, netted thousands of rabbits and a few coyote. The hunters shipped the carcasses to Denver to feed the poor. Hunters, both men and women, used guns and sometimes clubs to rid the area of these crop-destroying rodents. *Courtesy of Town of Haxtun.*

Harvest item about a Paoli hunt reported, "Jack rabbit hunts and roundups have been so numerous during the past few weeks that it has been pretty hard to keep track of all of them." The newspaper wrote that the hunts "varied in size and numbers of rabbits killed" but estimated hunters had killed around fifty thousand rabbits with more drives scheduled in the future. The hunters piled the rabbits near the railroad tracks for shipping to Denver, where they were dressed and donated to feed the poor.

In 1919, a number of enterprises operated in Dailey, including the Dailey Cooperative Company, the Dailey Garage and Blacksmith Shop, the Ridgway Brothers Garage, the Equity Mercantile Company and the Dailey State Bank, which opened in 1918. "Hence our town has grown in five years from nothing to a busy little burg of six business houses, eighteen dwellings and a population of about eighty-five," wrote Mabel Frank.

Emma Burke Conklin, writing in *A Brief History of Logan County*, called Dailey's progress remarkable. "The farms are well improved, the homes of the best type and the people are substantial and progressive."

The farmers near Dailey also kept busy. Mabel Frank noted that Edward W. Johnson purchased a quarter of land south of town in 1914 and has "taken up hog and cattle buying," O.K. Clark built a "modern bungalow equipped with electric lights and a heating plant" and X.A. Lambert "produces peaches, plums and cherries each year. His well-kept orchard is a sight beautiful to see."

Clark moved into Daily from his nearby farm in the early 1920s, constructed a new home and started the O.K. Garage, a Chevrolet dealership "that attracted many buyers and brought business to town," wrote Ross Frank.

With the DLD Highway bringing more cars through Dailey, gas stations opened on three corners of Main Street and other businesses opened as well during the early 1920s, including Foster Lumber Company, a leather shop and a blacksmith shop.

Formation of the Dailey Church began in 1921, with Reverend H.O. Jochens serving as pastor and holding services in the school. In July 1926, the Dailey congregation constructed a new building, with the first service held on August 1. "The new church represents a remarkable achievement for the Dailey community," wrote the *Harvest* on July 8, 1926. The newspaper credited Pastor Force with "helping to provide his congregation with a suitable church building—one of which any community might well be proud." The raising of funding and donated work meant the church would be nearly "debt free" by its dedication.

Dailey thrived into the early 1930s, its population reaching 150, before beginning its decline. Clark moved his Chevrolet dealership to Haxtun in 1928, and Foster Lumber and other businesses, including the Dailey Bank, closed. The bank closed its doors at noon on Monday, November 18, 1929, but the *Harvest* clarified "that the bank was not insolvent," and that "men who have inspected the last financial statement of the bank freely express the opinion that all depositors will receive their total deposits."

As the twenties ended and the thirties began, the Great Depression and the "dirty thirties" struck the Dailey farming community. The farmers found relief once their crops failed by hiring on to help build Highway 6, leasing their teams of horses for the task of grading the new highway. The empty Foster Lumber Company offered a stable for the horses and a mess hall for the workers. The men bunked in the vacant bank building.

A fire caused by an exploding presto tank destroyed the Dailey Farmers Cooperative Elevator in July 1933. The fire burned between 1,500 and 2,000 bushels of wheat, plus a "large amount of harness and other equipment" stored there after completion of Highway 6 between Haxtun and Fleming, reported the *Harvest*. Firefighters managed to carry the scale and day books kept on the counter out of the building, but a safe that went through the fire held the rest of company's books. "Owing to the intense heat of the pit where debris was burning for several hours after the fire, the safe had not yet been opened."

The newspaper explained that the gasoline engine used to elevate the grain was equipped with a presto tank. "Evidently the tank started leaking some time Sunday night" and ignited when elevator manager W.H. Smith started the engine on Monday morning. The article reported, "Almost instantly, the entire engine room was in flames and Smith had difficulty escaping." The fire spread quickly to the office, which "became a mass of flames" spread by an intense wind.

The call for help sounded the alarm at Haxtun, and a large number of firefighters responded to "join the bucket brigade that was instrumental in confining the fire to the elevator and preventing its spread to storage sheds on the east and west of the elevator." The fire attracted several hundred people from Haxtun and Dailey as word spread.

The Daily Post Office, which opened in 1916, closed on July 7, 1961, with mail dispatched out of Haxtun and Fleming. Mabel (Frank) Markham served as postmaster from the time the office opened until she retired in June 1960. The Dailey Church merged with the Haxtun United Methodist Church in 1967 because of low attendance and the inability to find a minister. The Dailey Elevator closed in 1985.

Fleming Develops at "29-Mile Siding"

During rainy periods, a lagoon formed in the center of the site that became the town of Fleming. Travelers on the Oregon Trail stopped there on their way to the South Platte River, but all moved on until 1885, when Russell Fulford and Frank Pratt took preempts nearby. A native of New York, Fulford left home at age fourteen in 1867 and spent the next eighteen years in Illinois and Nebraska working as a painter, decorator and sign writer. Pratt also grew up in New York but later moved to Hastings, Nebraska, where he worked as a painter and wallpaper hanger. With money from a winning lottery ticket, Pratt purchased a team of oxen and hooked them to Fulford's wagon, and the pair headed west to Colorado. According to *Memories of our Pioneers*, the men took preempts next to each other since no homesteads were available at that time. Preempts required filing intent, proof of occupancy and paying a small amount, usually $1.25 per acre for the land.

The CB&Q "High Line" Railroad left Holyoke in March 1887, placing water-tank stations at Paoli, Haxtun and a point twenty-six miles east of Sterling called "29-Mile Siding." When Logan County held its county seat election on December 20, 1887, 29-Mile Siding received eleven votes. Mail arrived at the siding addressed to "Calvert" in care of Railroad Superintendent Elwood Calvert of Lincoln, Nebraska, until July 27, 1888, when homesteader John McDonald petitioned the postmaster general to change the address to Fleming.

Calvert's brother-in-law Henry Bascom Fleming of Weeping Well, Nebraska, a representative of the Lincoln Land Company, received 240 acres of land one mile west of the siding from the railroad. On June 14, 1888, Fleming donated his land and surveyed a town site, which he platted as the "original Town of Fleming" on February 21, 1889.

Fleming's first businesses, according to the Fleming Historical Society, included a lumberyard, two loan companies, a barbershop, three general stores, a blacksmith shop, one attorney and two doctors who made house calls. During the 1890s depression and drought, Fleming nearly became a ghost town, but a new influx of settlers began arriving in 1904 and the town experienced a time of regrowth.

Winfield "Win" Morris settled three miles west of the siding in September 1886 and filed the first homestead patent in the area. Three years later in 1889, he married Annie Warren in Nebraska and started the *Fleming Herald* newspaper with his brother-in-law, Joe Reed. Win Morris later operated a hardware store and delivered mail to Fleming, Chenoa (located five miles south of Dailey) and LeRoy with his brother Cash Morris. The two took turns making the daily fifty-two-mile trip on horseback for a salary of twenty dollars per month.

Cash Morris, who opened Fleming's first hotel and restaurant, arrived from Syracuse, Nebraska, in 1887, traveling through Julesburg and across the sand hills in a "prairie schooner." He served as Logan County Commissioner for twenty-four years beginning in 1908, and through his efforts, Highway 6 came through Fleming rather than bypassing it.

E.P. Rogers of Pennsylvania started a stir in 1895, when he thought he "smelled crude oil" west of Fleming and convinced farmers, ranchers and railroad workers to buy stock in the Fleming Oil Company. He raised $735 to hire a hydraulic drilling rig owned by Charlie Harris, paying $1 per foot. Rogers lay down on his stomach each day sniffing for the oil. Conklin wrote that the train stopped each day to check the venture since many of the railroad workers owned stock. When the money ran out, the driller folded

Lew Knight and Ed Rudel's hardware store was located on the east side of Logan Avenue in Fleming, circa 1900s. The Methodist Church, Fleming's first church, sits in the background to the right of the store. *Courtesy of Reon Chaney.*

up his machine and left, and the investors went back to "farming, ranching and railroading." In 1910, Bert Vance found oil on his bit and on the ground while digging a well in that spot. A geologist confirmed it was oil but said that getting at it would be impossible.

Another geological phenomena occurred on the afternoon of January 14, 1904, at Galien, a railroad siding eight and one-half miles west of Fleming that consisted of a well with a stand tank, a pump house, a coal shed and a two-story section house. According to an account in *Memories of our Pioneers*, the sixteen-square-foot pump house covered a four-hundred-foot well with a ten-inch casing that sat on a solid formation at the bottom of the well. A six-foot high, six-hundred-pound steam engine sat on top of the casing. Twelve-by-twelve timbers crossed the well's eight-foot square border every sixteen feet to the bottom of the well to prevent a cave in. The engine's smokestack stood between thirty and fifty feet high. James Hradecky, a railroad section laborer, and his sister, Mary Hradecky, lived in the section house about one and one-half blocks from the pump house.

That day, Mary Hradecky, another brother John Hradecky and his fiancée, Mary Swedensky, took advantage of the warm afternoon to take a stroll. John, a section foreman, took a break from their walk to adjust the pump valve located sixteen feet below the ground inside the pump house while the two women waited outside. Once John finished checking the valve, he left the pump house, and the three started walking toward the section house. At that moment, they heard a noise that sounded like a fast approaching train and felt the earth shake. They turned to find the pump house with all its machinery missing, a fifty-foot gaping hole in its place. The railroad searched for the pump house, digging down seventy feet past the bottom of the hole, but never found the pump house or its contents. They ultimately ceased digging, filled the hole with dirt and left the mystery unsolved.

As settlers moved into the area during the early 1900s, Fleming once again thrived, and its citizens, then numbering 235, petitioned to incorporate on March 23, 1917. The subsequent special election seated councilmembers Grant Smith, Frank Fulford, W.B. Chamberlain, B.S. Munday, Edwin Davis, George Grauberger and Mayor Mike O'Leary. The council appointed Albert Worthley marshal, Ike R. Boyce deputy marshal, W.A. Brown clerk and J.W. Holmes treasurer.

At a general election held on April 2, 1918, voters turned down a $20,000 bond issue to fund the construction of a water works project for the town by fourteen to twenty-nine. The following year, the town came back to voters, this time seeking $40,000 for the project, and it passed fifty-one to one. The town added a curb and gutters in 1919 and, a few years later, constructed a plant to supply electricity. Fleming installed streetlights in 1938, updated its water and sewer system in 1952 and took over operation of the cemetery in 1958.

Another Morris brother, John Leslie Morris, who arrived in Fleming with his parents Mary and John Morris in 1893, helped organize the Farmers Bank of Fleming in 1917. He served as president from 1920 to 1947, when he retired and moved to Sterling. The bank changed its name to the First National Bank of Fleming and erected a new building in 1920. The cost of construction for the building included $1,200 to dig the basement, $14,000 for the building, $6,000 for furniture and fixtures and $830 for two vault doors.

In 1971, robbers cut through the bank's original vault doors with a special torch. Shortly after the robbery, the bank's owners considered moving it elsewhere but decided to call area residents to see if there was interest in keeping it in Fleming. Those calls raised enough new capital to renovate the interior and exterior of the bank. A new group of stockholders purchased the bank in 1977 and elected Wayne Scott president. The First National Bank of Fleming remains solvent and is the oldest bank in Logan County. "The investors kept it going, which tells you that you had some conservative farmers with some money even in hard times," said Scott.

Wayne Scott, who spent twelve years in banking, said Fleming had three banks at one time. The Commercial Bank, renamed Key Bank, moved to Sterling. The Fleming State Bank, opened in October 1914, went broke and closed in 1920.

By 1928, the population of Fleming reached five hundred, and its business community served a trade territory of fifteen miles in all directions. The list of enterprises included the town's light and water systems, Citizens Lumber and Supply Company, Logan Lumber Company, Frenchman Telephone Company, Farmers Cooperative Elevator Company, W.C. Harris Company Elevator, Fleming Elevator, Fulford Brothers blacksmith and implement, O'Leary Brothers Hardware, C.T. Gilbert Drugs, Fleming Mercantile Company, Charles Sparks's general merchandise store, Bushing Cash Store, Fleming Meat Market, Fleming Motel, Mrs. Della Gronnendyke's restaurant, Fleming Motor Company Garage, Reed and Crownenshield Garage, Rialto and Gem theaters and the *Fleming News*.

The road from Fleming to Sterling once took travelers across the South Platte River, sixteen miles over "Riordan Hill" and five and one-half miles north before reaching the DLD Highway, an all dirt road. Today Highway 6 makes travel to and from Sterling easier, allowing people to live in Fleming, while working and shopping in Sterling. Although few businesses remain in Fleming, its proud residents consider the town "a small part of a great nation." The Frenchman School District, one of the best in the area and a source of pride for the town, draws students from Sterling and the surrounding area. In addition to the bank and Grainland Cooperative, Fleming is home to Bully's Pub, famous for Rocky Mountain oysters, steak and seafood, which draws customers from all directions.

Chapter Four

FARMING

Horses to the Age of Power

The first influx of homesteaders to northeastern Colorado found a welcoming land in which to develop farming, as the mid-1880s experienced an unusual amount of rainfall. Wild grapes, elderberries, currants, wild vegetables, native grasses and sagebrush covered the prairie. Land speculators, newspapers and the railroads sang the praises of this "prairie rain belt." An 1887 railroad pamphlet declared, "So much rain now falls in the eastern portion of Colorado that it is no longer fit for a winter range for cattle."

The High Plains presented challenges, but homesteaders met each with enthusiasm. Win Morris claimed he enjoyed plowing sod amid "cactus and rattlesnakes" and walking barefoot to carry water from the Platte River through land so barren and indistinguishable that he took all his belongings with him, fearing that he would not be able to find his way back to his homestead.

Farmers faced natural menaces like prairie fires, tornadoes, hail and grasshoppers. One settler described an 1887 invasion of grasshoppers that looked "like clouds, carrying destruction before them; silver winged, and in the sunlight appearing like silver dollars."

Despite these obstacles, farming worked well until the rain stopped in 1890. Wilbur Kipp heard stories about those drought years, the worst in 1892. He said, "There was not one blade of grass out there."

In 1894, only six inches of rain fell and the only other moisture came from snow driven by wind so strong that it destroyed farm buildings and killed livestock gathered for protection along barbwire fences. An April 1895 blizzard delayed a Union Pacific train traveling from Julesburg to Denver for eighteen hours. Adding to the adversity, a depression caused by the 1893 banking panic swept the nation, dropping the price of grain below the cost of production. The drought lingered for nearly ten years, and after the second and third season with no rain and low prices, many homesteaders gave up and left. Towns shrank in size, and county populations dwindled.

Those who stayed, either out of determination or necessity, found ways beyond farming to stave off starvation. The *Logan County Ledger* relates how Crook pioneer J.M. Lynch traveled to Haxtun in 1891 to trade antelope for corn, receiving ten bushels per animal. He also killed wolves, earning a bounty of two dollars for each from the county treasurer. Other homesteaders survived by finding work elsewhere.

Ruby (Riley) Heaston, whose mother—Alice Olson—came to the area in 1890 with her parents, John H. and Cynthia Olson, talked to me about her grandparents' struggle to hold onto their farm during a 1990 interview: "I remember hearing stories about [how], one year, my grandfather walked to Greeley to work." John Olson built the first grain elevator in Haxtun.

Many farmers survived through diversification. In 1892, local farmers sought markets for potatoes and cabbage. Talk of sugar beets began as early as 1898, when the *State Herald* announced that "every farmer in Phillips County who desires to plant eight acres of sugar beets could get two pounds of free seed." A *State Herald* news item on March 27, 1903, reported that the Haxtun area contracted to raise two hundred and twenty-six acres of sugar beets. In November, a Mr. White shipped 150 tons of sugar beets to the Eaton sugar factory. Others planted broomcorn, a variety of sorghum with stiff stalks used to make brooms. Wilbur Groves, a prominent Haxtun farmer, whose granddaughter owns the Bible Lighthouse in Sterling, grew cane that made "fine sorghum and stock feed." Encouraged by intermittent showers in 1894, a few farmers who planned to leave decided to stay, but the crops did not materialize that year either. Some left but held onto their land, coming back when the drought ended. Despite the setbacks during the 1890s, a second influx of settlers arrived during the first decade of the new century. By spring 1916, farmers broke between three and four thousand acres of sod and ten times that much by 1919.

Wayne Scott, whose grandparents—A.C. "Archie" and Sophie Scott—purchased land northwest of Haxtun in 1909, explained why many of those first homesteaders left in defeat: "A lot of the original settlers came from Nebraska and Iowa where the farming methods were completely different than was needed in this area. Those people all used surface planters because they were used to farming where there was abundant moisture. Later settlers used a lister, which created a furrow with ridges along each side of the row. They then dropped the seed into the furrow and used a disk to cover it up." He said that method helped retain the moisture.

In 1919, the *Harvest* reported 877 farms under cultivation in Phillips County, with acreage production "better than ever" for corn and other grains. Although wind and dust storms caused some spotted fields and cool nights "retarded the growth of straw," the *Harvest* predicted that the only thing that could hamper the expected "record crop" would be hail, another constant threat to farming on the High Plains.

Farm size increased between 1910 and 1920, especially in the non-irrigated parts of the state. The average size farm in Phillips County in 1921 was 270 acres. Production on these larger farms created a need for storage, and in August 1922, two shifts of laborers worked to complete a new elevator at Haxtun to handle that year's wheat crop.

While the number of Colorado farms decreased in 1923, especially on the eastern Plains, established northeastern Colorado farmers raising livestock, poultry, dairy cattle and hogs increased their holdings. A record corn crop fed the increasing number of hogs and dairy cattle that year.

Haxtun's Cooper Hog Ranch, owned by Duroc Livestock Company of Denver and considered one of the largest in the world, purchased much of the corn grown in Phillips and the surrounding counties, paying two cents above market. The operation, located on the east edge of Haxtun south of the railroad tracks and considered the most modern type of the time, sat on sixty-five acres, forty of those used for pens and buildings, including office space. The facility, which employed around fifteen men and shipped around twenty thousand hogs annually, could house five thousand hogs at one time.

The Haxtun yard stored grain in its own elevator, ground and mixed its own feed and supplied its own water using a modern pumping plant. The company purchased 65,000 bushels of corn in 1922 and doubled that in 1923.

Hogs and cream shipments in late August 1923 made up for a decrease in wheat shipments, and that same year, the railroad began construction of new stockyards to accommodate the increased cattle and hog shipments. In June 1924, the Burlington Northern Railroad agency reported ninety cars of grain, cattle, hogs and cream with a value of $100,000 shipped out of Haxtun. The *Harvest* noted that hogs accounted for twenty-four of the loads and that cream shipments doubled from the previous year.

A business that provided a local market for dairy producers opened in 1933. The B&B Cheese Factory operated in Haxtun until March 1937, when owner C.H. Baker moved the equipment to his Sterling plant with a promise that the company would continue to contract for milk from local dairy herds. The plant purchased whole milk, but when the spread between the price for cream and that paid by the cheese factory for whole milk became minimal, farmers opted to separate the cream from the milk.

Over the years, the number of acres planted to corn, spring wheat, oats, dry beans and grain sorghums steadily grew, and by 1932, corn replaced the fall wheat crop on most farms. The number of acres planted with barley and potatoes decreased, although most farmers continued to grow potatoes for their own use.

Farming in the early 1900s required long, strenuous days for the entire family. Farmers cut wheat with a horse-drawn binder, stacked the bundles on a horse-drawn wagon and then hauled the bundles to a steam-powered thrashing machine with an incessant thirst for water. Workers filled the thrasher's tank wagon, also pulled by horses, from a water tank that stayed busy running back and forth from the water source to the steam engine. A separate container of water stood by for the thirsty field hands.

It took ten to fifteen families working together to feed the bundles and fuel to the thrashing machine as it moved from farm to farm. The machine's engine burned corncobs and coal. It took gentle horses to pull the wagon

In the early 1900s, farmers cut wheat with a horse-drawn binder and then stacked the bundles on a horse-drawn wagon before hauling it to a steam-powered thrashing machine like Ab Fleming's thrashing outfit pictured here. *Courtesy of Reon Chaney.*

used to haul the harvested grain along side the moving belts. "Farming back then was a slow process," Ruby Heaston's husband, Fred, told me in 1990. Fred Heaston learned about early farming from his father-in-law Irwin Riley and from his own experience. According to Heaston, "We spent all summer doing something, working from sunup to sundown."

Harvesters picked corn by hand and tossed it into a wagon equipped with a "bank" board (a high board that kept the ears from flying over the side) and pulled by horses trained to move a short distance before waiting for the pickers, who harvested two rows at a time. Pickers wore a pair of corn shucking mittens with a stall to protect the thumb and a shucking hook on the right hand. Left-handed pickers wore the shucking hook on the left hand and moved around the field counterclockwise. The corn stalks fed cattle and horses turned loose in the fields once harvest ended. Corn harvest began in October, said Fred Heaston. "Sometimes, if you were lucky, you finished by Thanksgiving."

Women helped pick corn but also kept house, raised children and fed the harvest crews. Clara Bjorklun, in *Those Were the Days*, recalled getting up before daylight, cooking breakfast for five men in addition to her own family, getting her children ready for the school bus and then picking corn.

Ruby Heaston recounted the long days of cooking: "By the time they got the horses harnessed you were supposed to have breakfast on the table. After you fed them breakfast, you started cooking lunch and when that was over, you started supper. After supper, you started getting stuff ready for breakfast again."

"We ate a lot in those days, and I guess a lot of it was fat food," said Fred Heaston. "But I can tell you we worked it off."

Once harvested, farmers stored the corn in a wire hoop or corncrib until winter, when a corn sheller arrived to separate the kernels from the cobs,

After picking corn by hand, farmers stored the ears in corncribs to await the sheller that would separate the kernels from the cobs. As workers fed ears into the sheller, they separated the best for planting the following season. This photo, taken around 1910, shows the old Farmers Cooperative Elevator in the background at right. *Courtesy of Reon Chaney.*

which provided fuel along with wood and coal to heat homes. Neighbors helped each other scoop the corn ears into the sheller, with the best ears sorted and kept for seed to plant the next season. The kernels went into corn bins for storage or into wagons to haul to town to sell.

Fleming-area farmer Paul Etl started farming with horses, using two, three or four animals, depending on the machinery. He opined that two horses pulling a lister plowed straighter rows. After the feed grew a couple of weeks, three horses hitched to a three-section "harrow" drug the dirt and rolled it toward the plants to cover up small weeds. When the corn or feed grew to a couple of feet tall, they used a "go-dig" to level the ridges and kill any new weeds. He remembered, "It was hard to keep from covering up the crop."

Fred Heaston recalled that a two-row lister pulled by six horses planted about twenty-five acres per day.

The Age of Power

The mechanics of agriculture progressed rapidly during the first one hundred years of American history, and by the 1890s, when farming spread across the High Plains, the steel gangplow had replaced the one-bottom wooden plow; the reaper had replaced the scythe and cradle; and the cultivator had replaced the handheld hoe. The corn planter, hay press and twine grain binder made farming easier, but horses, oxen or mules remained the common power. Portable steam engines replaced some animal power in the 1850s, but horses pulled those machines from site to site.

Horses were so essential to early agriculture that their breeding became a science with draft horses rated on thirty-five items, according to a 1911 scorecard. Horses that passed with high scores brought top prices, and even during the 1890s bad farming economy, a 1,800-pound draft horse brought $260 in Chicago. Five breeds—Percheron, Clydesdale, Shire, Belgian and Suffolk—dominated the market.

Even these large breeds had limited strength, requiring farmers to own numerous horses to get the needed power. Feeding and caring for these animals added to farm chores. A government study found that it took twenty-seven minutes per day to care for each horse, a total of six hours per day for a dozen horses. It also took millions of acres to grow feed for these power sources. Fred Heaston stopped farming with horses in the 1940s. "I

An early Avery combine pulled by a Rumely "oil-pull" tractor, circa 1920s, appeared modern compared to horse power, but the going remained slow. *Courtesy of Reon Chaney.*

liked farming with horses despite the fact that it was tedious," he said, " but tractors worked better."

Fewer than 1,000 United States farmers owned tractors in 1910, but that number increased to 25,000 by 1915 and 158,000 by 1919. It was not until the 1920s, with the introduction of the two- and three-plow general-purpose tractors, that tractor power became practical for the typical farmer. The first two-cylinder, kerosene-powered tractor, the Waterloo Boy, used from 1916 to 1924, featured a combined pressure feed and splash lubrication system with a pump, fan and radiator cooling system. It also came with a cone clutch, open spur gear and pinion final drive. Forward speed reached two and a quarter miles per hour. Although ruggedness, efficiency and operational factors improved steadily, the two-cylinder engine, called "two-luggers" or "poppin' Johnies" remained popular until the 1960s.

Rubber tires replaced steel wheels in the 1930s, but many farmers remained leery of their ability to move unhindered in fields until experience convinced them.

By the 1960s, larger farms required more power than the dependable two-cylinder engine could offer. Thus began the "age of power": tractors with power steering, four-wheel drive, fuel efficiency, twenty-four-speed transmissions, cushioned-suspension seats and enclosed cabs with air conditioning. Fred Heaston recalled when he thought an umbrella represented comfort.

McCormick-Deering manufactured this Number Eight Harvester-Thresher, which International Harvester later called a "combine," in the mid- to late 1920s. While a tractor often pulled the harvester, horses continued to pull the wagons carrying the grain. *Courtesy of Reon Chaney.*

Besides comfort, today's tractor also comes with a high-tech control panel that alerts harvesters of possible problems with the machine or the field. These modern tractors offer power and convenience but come with a much higher price tag. A tractor today costs between $300,000 and $350,000, depending on features and size.

When Rex Hadeen went to work for Miller Implement in Haxtun in 1948, a thirty-six-horse-power tractor cost around $1,000. "A farmer could take three loads of wheat to market and get enough money to buy a good tractor," Hadeen told me in 1990.

In the late 1930s, the mechanical corn picker started replacing hand pickers, but the corn sheller remained in use until the late 1950s, when the combine took over the task. Although the mechanical picker lessened the chore of picking corn, it came with dangers. "Many farmers lost fingers and even hands when they stopped to remove weeds from the picker's rollers," said Hadeen. The first mechanical combine, a Massy Harris with a twelve-foot header, made the corn picker obsolete. Today's combines—many with the same comforts, power and digital capabilities as the modern tractor—can be adapted to cut small grains such as wheat, milo, oats and barley. They also harvest corn and sunflowers.

Pull-type swathers, used to lay down crops such as alfalfa, forage feed, hay and straw for baling, became self-propelled in the mid-1950s. Farmers cut these crops green and leave them to dry before baling. The first balers packed the cut crop into eighty- to ninety-pound square bales, which they loaded by hand onto a trailer for transfer to storage. Most farmers converted to round balers that pack the crop into round bales weighing upwards of two thousand pounds in the 1970s.

Farming equipment changes to keep up with changing farming techniques, said Wayne Scott. "Machinery companies work with the farmers to develop the machinery to do what needs to be done."

Water, a Coveted Resource

From the beginning, water became a coveted commodity. When possible, homesteaders located their farms near a surface water source such as a creek, but since that was not always possible, most hauled water by loading barrels onto wagons pulled by horses until they could dig a well. Ernest Thimmigans, who homesteaded by a creek near LeRoy in Logan County in 1889, used "witching" to locate the place to dig his well and struck water quickly. Witching entailed the use of a willow rod a few feet long with two prongs made by cutting off the branches. The "witcher" holds the rod loosely in one hand with the stake end up and walks across the area. Thimmigans dug his well at the place where the stake suddenly pulled toward the ground, and it provided sufficient water for household, stock and garden use for many years.

Digging a well by hand took considerable work. In 1898, Washington Slay recorded the progress of his hand-dug well:

> *February 12: We got well down 64 feet.*
> *February 14: We got the well down to 100 feet.*
> *February 15: Well down to 122 feet, had considerable trouble with the rock and sand caving in while we were drilling.*
> *February 16: We got down to 144 feet but struck sand.*
> *February 18: We put the corking down and bored about four or five feet.*

February 19: We got down 160 feet.

February 21: We found water at 175 feet and got the curbing down to within 16 feet of the water.

February 22: Jack, Bernard and I worked on the well all day, was bothered considerably by rock, got the tube down to 156 feet.

February 23: The well is 176 feet deep with six and one-half feet of water from four feet rim of good coarse water gravel.

February 24: John Olson and I put the pump in the well.

The railroad dug the first wells to provide water tank stations. Towns like Holyoke, Paoli, Haxtun, Dailey and Fleming developed at those stations, but later, the towns dug wells of their own to serve growing populations. Haxtun dug its first well by hand in 1923. Eventually capped, the worker's log leaves a record of the types of soils found during the digging as well as the implements used in the progress. The well hole measured five feet in circumference. The worker used a spade to dig the first twelve feet then ran into "yellow sandy loam" to a depth of twenty feet where he struck a "hard red formation" that required blasting and a pick for the next thirty-five feet. At around fifty-six feet, the worker reached "blue clay" and returned to using a spade.

Continuing to dig with the spade, he reached gravel at sixty-three feet and water seeping through the gravel at seventy feet. After two feet of clay, continuing to use the spade, he found nine feet of gravel before reaching another five feet of clay. Below that clay, he encountered a layer of hard sandstone that required the use of a pick.

He dug through two additional layers of gravel that had "rock sledge" below them before reaching red clay at 110 feet. The red clay gave way to sand at 170 feet and then "coarse gravel" for 8 feet before hitting "rock sledge" again.

As the number of wells increased, farmers began looking for ways to use this underground water source for irrigation. The *State Herald* reported on September 10, 1897, that a group from Denver would be in Holyoke to put in a test irrigation plant using compressed air to pull water from wells.

Farmers considered running pipelines from the Republican River in Nebraska in 1902 and from the Narrows Reservoir near Fort Morgan in 1910, but the estimated cost of this latter project—which proposed damming the South Plate River to irrigate one million acres in Weld, Logan and Phillips Counties—was $25 million.

While these ideas failed, mostly due to lack of financing, attempts at using groundwater through wells continued, and in 1937, Joe Paloucek and

Burt Randall, both farming southwest of Holyoke, recorded irrigation wells that used a flooding method. It was not until the 1960s with the invention of sprinklers and the formation of water districts under the Groundwater Management Act that the number of irrigation wells increased, with four hundred dug from 1963 through 1976 in what became the Frenchman Groundwater Management District.

Judge A.C. Adams appointed the first board of directors for the Frenchman Groundwater Management District once the state approved its formation on May 18, 1967. They included Erwin Heermann, Clyde Sperber and Billy Sprague of Holyoke; Ward Dee and Lorin Starkebaum of Haxtun; and Julius Wernsman of Fleming.

Darrell Phillips of Phillips Drilling Company drilled many of those four hundred wells. In a 1990 interview with me, Phillips related that there was a "flurry" during those years to drill wells because there was only so much water and a limit on the number of wells allowed: "It was phenomenal. I drilled solid for two years before we had to go in and rebuild our equipment. There was such a demand."

The first "high-angle" sprinkler systems used all-water drives hooked to high-pressure water pumps and required eighty to one hundred pounds of pressure to operate. Today's "low-angle" sprayers cost less to operate and shoot closer to the ground, conserving water because the wind does not catch it and carry it off.

Chapter Five

PRAIRIE BECOMES DUST BOWL

Soil Conservation District Formed

After three decades of rain and plowing, drought returned to the High Plains in the 1930s, and when thirsty crops died, the prairie winds scooped up the bare, unanchored topsoil and swirled it for miles. Jack Falk witnessed his first dust storm in second grade: "I watched it come in the window of the school room. It was absolutely black."

While the northeast corner of Colorado lies just outside the area officially designated as the "Dust Bowl," the area did not escape the phenomena. "We got pure red soil from Oklahoma," said Wilbur Kipp. "We didn't have the same problems that they had at Eads, Kit Carson and Burlington where they went down and broke out ash powder soil. Here, the soil was broken out too, but it didn't leave the country." Regardless of where the dust came from, it created havoc: "It was so dark that we had to turn the lights on, and the wind was blowing so bad that the hanging lights were swaying. It didn't rain but it sprinkled mud balls that hit the windows."

In March 1934, the *Harvest* reported that the dry air created enough static electricity to stall two hundred cars near Broomfield, and in June, "wind and dust storms" took a toll on crops, with the greatest damage to corn. The wind filled lister furrows, covering young corn plants with "loose, dry dust." The velocity of the wind overturned small buildings. "Practically every home in this section is full of fine dust," wrote the *Harvest*. Older settlers likened the wind and dry weather to the drought of 1894: "Pastures throughout this section are very short and some farmers are moving their livestock great distances in an effort to find pasture."

The dust blew during winter as well, and in February 1935, a "typical spring blizzard" created a "fog of dust," reported the *Harvest*. The town of Haxtun turned on the streetlights so people could "discern objects across the street." The following week, a second blizzard arrived, "trailing two dust storms," followed by swirling snow. "Although the snow was fairly heavy in the entire region, fields in general were deprived of the moisture due to drifting. Fences, weed patches and buildings accumulated large drifts," leaving the open ground "practically barren." The temperatures dropped below zero over the weekend, but warm weather returned, melting the snow and turning Haxtun's dirt streets to mud.

John Wolfe of Fleming recalled sand blowing over the top of the fence rows and wet blankets hanging on the outside of doors and windows to keep the dust from coming into the house. Wolfe attended a funeral one day in 1935 at which mourners turned on their automobile lights to drive because it was "pitch dark" due to the blowing dust.

Adding to the drought conditions, the entire country suffered from a depression brought on by the October 29, 1929 stock market crash (Black Tuesday). "The drought went right along with the Depression," said Wayne Scott. "If we wouldn't have had the drought in the 1930s, the farm people around here probably would not have been affected by the Depression like they were in the cities because every farmer had a few milk cows, a few chickens and a few hogs, and they actually ate out of their backyard."

Wayne's wife, Doris Scott, says people get confused about the Depression and the drought: "The Depression hit the people in the east, and the drought and the Depression hit here. So, we had a double whammy."

When the Depression and drought hit in the 1930s, Wayne's grandparents, Archie and Sophie Scott, owed $4,000 on their farm. Archie offered his youngest son, Lyle (Wayne's father), half the farm if he would stay to help get them through the Depression and save the farm. "That scenario played out many times, where someone was on the verge of losing the farm but stubbornness and determination kicked in," said Wayne. "The farm was the focal point of life. Everything had to be for the farm. Some people didn't have that focus, and they didn't stay. They just didn't want to fight."

Lyle Scott hauled corn to Greeley to make money during the 1930s. He also worked at the sugar factory and Wayne's mother, Jessie (Whitney) Scott, raised chickens to help meet expenses.

Wilbur Kipp's parents, Clarence and Agnes Kipp, also did what they could to survive. "Everybody was just so hard up," said Wilbur. "The only guys who could raise anything were the guys north of town in the sand. The hard land (south of town) would just burn up." The drought was so bad that farmers had to import alfalfa hay to feed cattle: "They wanted a dollar a bale for it. Well, nobody had a dollar."

NEW DEAL FOR AMERICA'S FARMERS AND SOIL CONSERVATION

With the election of Franklin D. Roosevelt in 1932 came the New Deal and the creation of three agencies to assist farmers: the Civilian Conservation Corps (CCC), the Soil Conservation Service (SCS) and the Resettlement Administration (RA).

The CCC employed young, unskilled and unmarried men between the ages of eighteen and twenty-five to perform labor related to conservation and development of natural resources. In eastern Colorado, the CCC worked with the SCS to construct earth dams, soil terraces and contour furrows. They also planted range vegetation and trees while living in military-style camps, where they received shelter, clothing, food and a small wage of thirty dollars per month—twenty-five of which the agency sent home to the family.

The RA initiated changes in land use slated for restoration, made loans to farmers, encouraged conservation practices to rehabilitate the soil and purchased farmland to take it out of production. The establishment of the United States Department of Agriculture (USDA) in 1935 changed the RA's focus to running the Standard Rural Rehabilitation Loan Program, a predecessor of the Farmers Home Administration, renamed the Farm Security Administration in 1937.

Two additional pieces of legislation passed in 1933 offered farmers assistance. The Emergency Farm Mortgage Act established the Farm Credit System (FCS) of cooperative lending institutions to provide short-, intermediate- and long-term loans for agriculture. On February 12, 1934, representatives from five northeastern Colorado counties—Sedgwick, Phillips, Yuma, Washington and Logan—met in Sterling to incorporate the Sterling Production Credit Association under the FCS. The first temporary board included F. Parker of Julesburg, Steven J. Meakins of Haxtun, Harry W. McKinney of Yuma, Ezra Alishouse of Akron and Sam Bennison of Sterling.

The Agricultural Adjustment Administration (AAA) paid farmers subsidies for leaving a portion of their land fallow and killing off excess livestock, with the purpose of reducing surpluses and raising value. The government supported these subsidies by taxing companies that processed farm products. In December 1933, 900 Phillips County farmers signed contracts under the AAA's wheat allotment and production control program. By the following January, the number increased to 1,400. These farmers received $115,000 in subsidies for land kept out of production that season.

The corn-hog plan came to Phillips County in the beginning of 1934, when farmers agreed to cut their corn acreage by twenty percent and hog raisers agreed to reduce litters farrowed to three-fourths of the previous year's average. The corn growers received thirty cents per bushel for land contracted to the government and the hog raisers received five dollars per head. More than seven hundred farmers signed corn-hog contracts with anticipation of receiving nearly $150,000 in payments.

In January 1936, the United States Supreme Court declared the Agricultural Adjustment Act unconstitutional because it "invalidated the rights of states." While some farmers voiced a protest and others considered it a "boon," most farmers agreed on the need for a substitution for the AAA. President Roosevelt signed a new agricultural adjustment program in March 1935, authorizing $500 million in subsidies annually for farmers to withdraw land from crop production and for "soil building growth or other economic purposes." The money went directly to farmers or through states to set up "approved conservation programs," with the goal to take thirty thousand acres of land out of production in 1936.

A new Agricultural Adjustment Act in 1938 reorganized the USDA; made changes in conservation, crop support and marketing legislation; and gave the federal government more control over decisions made by the American farmer. Wayne Scott said the new AAA worked well, but he was not sure about the farm programs that came later: "At the time everybody signed up, but in retrospect, looking back, we would have probably been a lot better off if we had never seen a farm program. I think it held the prices down all of those years rather than bolstering them."

Reon Chaney, who farms north of Haxtun, feels differently: "Whatever the government wanted me to do, I did because I knew that was where the money was."

Even as High Plains farmers struggled to "save the farm" from financial disaster, they understood that "saving the soil" was vital for long-term survival. Congress started the process in 1930, when the Buchanan Amendment to the Agricultural Appropriation Bill provided $160,000 to study soil erosion. President Roosevelt appointed H.H. "Hugh" Bennett, considered the father of soil conservation, to head a new Soil Erosion Service to demonstrate projects around the country. The Soil Erosion Service became the Soil Conservation Service (SCS) in 1936.

When Charles Erickson made his way on foot from the Julesburg train station to his homestead in 1885, he walked through the tall grass growing north of Haxtun but settled south of there, where the shorter grass would be easier to break out, not realizing the implications of the taller grass. "I always said if I ever farmed it wouldn't be south of the railroad tracks," said Wilbur Kipp. He explained that water runs off the hard soil found south of town while moisture flows through the sandy loam found to the north, settling in the clay subsoil. The tall grass that Erickson walked through was an indication of the moisture retentive properties of that clay subsoil.

Sandy or hard soil mattered little when it rained, but farmers soon learned that High Plains rain could be fickle. In the aftermath of the Dust Bowl, those who managed to hold on to their land realized they must learn better methods of retaining the area's precious moisture. The SCS played a major role in putting those better methods into practice.

Four men—Wally Bruce, Chuck Allen, Jack Falk and Merlyn "Pink" Queen—figure into the history of soil conservation in northeast Colorado. Wally Bruce studied soils at the University of Nebraska before taking a job with the conservation survey division at his alma mater in a training capacity, earning one dollar per day. That training in western Nebraska prepared him for the role he eventually played in soil conservation in Colorado, first in Cheyenne Wells and, later, in the northeast corner of the state.

Bruce reached Cheyenne Wells during the summer of 1935, working as a soil scientist. Fifty years later, he recalled those early days of soil conservation as a time when the government applied demonstration projects with permission from the farmer. "That philosophy failed because the farmer felt uninvolved," said Bruce in a 1985 interview with me. "It was his land, but he didn't have any part of it." Later policy changed to allow the farmer to perform the work while the SCS gave technical advice. Everyone was still learning about the Plains, said Bruce. "Some predicted that it would take fifty years to bring back the grass, but as soon as the rain came, those grasses started to respond." To hasten the process, the SCS applied measures such as contour furrows and ridges to hold the water in the field.

The Farm Forestry Service moved into the Haxtun Town Hall in August 1941, with the goal of setting up forestry plans in the northwest corner of Phillips County and the southeast section of Logan County. Farmers could choose to follow a conservation plan coordinated by the farmer and the SCS or to follow a farm forestry plan.

When Bruce advanced to the position of conservationist in 1942, his area included all of northeastern Colorado, and he moved his headquarters from Denver to Haxtun Town Hall. His responsibilities, in addition to soil conservation, included overseeing the planting of trees through CCC projects, one of those a windbreak in Dailey.

The SCS struggled to gain acceptance because farmers remained leery of government mandates. However, in 1946, Haxtun farmer Louis Koch made a trip to Washington, D.C., to testify about the need for a program at Haxtun. With encouragement from Koch, Bruce petitioned an election to form the Haxtun Soil Conservation District (HSCD), which included township seven and part of township eight in Logan County and townships six and seven in Phillips County. The original HSCD contained 122,100 acres, but over the next year, other landowners petitioned to include their land, increasing the acreage to 138,040.

When farmers and ranchers in the remaining parts of Phillips County, northern Yuma County and eastern Logan County wanted to bring their land into the HSCD, the board held a referendum, which approved the entry of all land within Phillips County and township six in Logan County unless an individual requested exclusion. This brought the district's acres to over 500,000 by the time Orville F. Freeman, secretary of agriculture 1961–69, signed an updated Memorandum of Understanding in 1963. The first officers of the HSCD board included President Louis Koch, Vice-President Keith Bunker and Secretary-Treasurer Henry Lambert.

Bruce hired Chuck Allen in 1952 to serve as conservationist while he oversaw the nine counties of the Northeast Colorado District. Allen grew up at Briggsdale, where he developed an interest in soil conservation while working in the Land Use program. After college at Colorado Agriculture College (later Colorado State University) in Fort Collins, he spent time in the United States Army before taking a position at Joe's overseeing on-the-job training for veterans. Finding that job unsatisfactory because "the veterans knew more than he did," Allen welcomed the offer to work as conservationist at Haxtun when it came in 1952. The SCS transferred Allen to Byers in 1965, but he returned to Haxtun in 1975 and retired there in 1983. Chuck Allen died in 1995.

Wally Bruce moved to Sterling and Byers for a time but returned to Haxtun in 1965. He spent his final year with the SCS as research conservationist for the six counties of Sedgwick, Phillips, Logan, Morgan,

Washington and Yuma. He retired in February 1976, continuing to live in Haxtun until he died in a car accident in October 1989.

Jack Falk grew up on a farm in the Fairfield Community, graduated from Haxtun High School in 1945 and then enrolled at CSU in Fort Collins to study general agriculture until a call from the military put an end to his studies. He returned to the area once he completed his military duty and began farming and hauling gas for Continental Oil.

The SCS still operated out of its office at Haxtun Town Hall when Falk reported for work on September 15, 1959, his thirty-second birthday, and began sharing the tiny office with Chuck Allen. "He had a desk and I had a table," said Falk in a 2001 interview. "We had a couple file cabinets and a storage cabinet and that was about it." Falk and Allen worked out of the town hall until the summer of 1961, when the HSCD purchased a small stucco building located on Highway 6 from the Haxtun Cooperative.

Following Allen's retirement from the SCS in 1983, Merlyn "Pink" Queen moved into the position as conservationist at Haxtun. Queen grew up in Crook, where he graduated from high school in 1963. After high school, he attended Northeastern Junior College in Sterling and later CSU in Fort Collins, where he graduated in 1967. To help pay for college, he took summer employment working in soil conservation districts at Fleming, Akron and Haxtun, where he met Jack Falk.

Two years in Vietnam interrupted Queen's career, but he ultimately took a job with the SCS, spending time in Greeley, Wray, Yuma and Las Animas before coming to Haxtun in 1984. "I always liked the Haxtun district," said Queen. "So, I was hoping it was for a long time." Queen remained with the SCS in Haxtun until he retired in 1998. He continues to make Haxtun his home.

The Phillips County Soil Survey, completed in the mid-1960s and published in 1971, shows three types of soil in Phillips County. The "hard land," covering 72 percent of the county, is "nearly level to gently sloping" with a loam surface layer and clay loam to clay subsoil. The "sandy land" consists of "level to gently sloping soils that have a sandy loam or loamy sand surface layer and sandy loam to clay loam subsoil." This type of soil covers 19 percent of the county, with the largest area surrounding Haxtun, mostly to the north. A third type of "rolling to hilly soils" of "fine sand" are found in the southeast corner of the county, where native grasses continue to grow for grazing. By 1964, nearly 6,400 acres of Phillips County land were irrigated, with the rest range or dry-farmed cropland. The major crops produced on irrigated land are sugar beets and corn.

Three types of sandy soil—Haxtun, Julesburg and Valent—dominate the area north of Dailey and Fleming in Logan County, according to the Logan County Soil Survey completed between 1965 and 1974. The "deep and well drained" Haxtun and Julesburg soils found on farms just north of Fleming and Dailey provide grazing or grow nonirrigated crops such as wheat and millet. A few farms use sprinkler irrigation to grow corn and alfalfa. The potential is poor for growing crops in the "deep and excessively drained" Valent soil found farther north and west.

A semiarid climate with "low humidity, wide variations in precipitation and temperatures and abundant sunshine" characterizes the northeastern Colorado High Plains, with an average annual precipitation of seventeen inches. The SCS Great Plains Conservation Program (GPCP), established in 1956, created a cost-share system for participating in conservation practices. From its beginning through 1985, the GPCP established plant cover on 5 million acres of cropland, planted over 65,000 acres of windbreaks, developed strip cropping on 1 million acres of land and built 15,000 miles of pipelines to carry water to livestock. USDA paid contracted participants 50 to 80 percent of the cost for each approved practice.

Jack Falk, who retired from SCS in 1994, came out of retirement in 1997 to take a part-time position as manager of the HSCD. He said many people confuse the service with the district. The SCS, now the Natural Resources and Conservation Service (NRCS), is a federal program that provides funding for conservation programs slated at improving and protecting soil, water and wildlife habitat. The HSCD, which organized under state government, is responsible for designing conservation plans.

Falk retired again in 2001, this time with emotion. The SCS rented the building from HSCD until April 1, 1999, when a federal order mandated that the service move to Holyoke to share office space with the Farm Service Agency. Falk refers to that day as "April Fool's Day 1999."

The district fought hard to keep the office in Haxtun, where it was formed and operated for fifty-three years, but the federal bureaucracy refused to budge. The move meant farther travel for many of the farmers, especially those in Logan County, who participated in HSCD services but applied for other farm programs in Sterling rather than Holyoke. In an effort to keep the office in Haxtun, the HSCD board offered to provide the office space rent-free, but when the end came on January 5, 2001, Roy Hall, conservationist with NRCS, told me, "Nobody cares what it costs [to relocate the office] because it has no impact on the situation." The situation was that USDA wanted "one-stop" shopping.

A Caterpillar D2 Tractor, introduced in 1938, pulls a lister plow to prepare a field for planting. Most farmers today leave the stubble in the field, using it as moisture-retaining mulch, rather than tilling the soil. *Courtesy of Reon Chaney.*

While Jack Falk believes all of the practices initiated by the SCS helped, he said the practice of conservation tillage (no-till) used today could solve soil erosion for the future. The debris left on the field in no-till farming acts as mulch on the undisturbed soil while chemicals control the weeds. "These days if a field is blowing it means someone got careless," said Falk

Wayne Scott started using no-till in 1990: "It was very new. I looked at it and watched it for a few years and then I started using it. Everybody gradually went to it and now just about everybody uses that technique."

"When I first started farming, I would go out and list the whole thing. Big mistake," said Wilbur Kipp, adding that he tried other practices but never got control of the land until he started using no-till farming. "We just plant on the surface leaving as much trash as we can. You plant right in the stubble and the stubble protects the moisture. We have learned a lot."

Chapter Six

ROBBERY, MURDER AND OTHER CRIMES

On the afternoon of February 25, 1915, Henry Schennegee, alias William Thompson, walked into the Farmers State Bank of Haxtun, emerged a short time later—carrying a grain sack filled with $5,000 in currency, gold and silver—and left assistant cashier John Brunke dying in the bank's vault. Next-day accounts in the *State Herald*, *Holyoke Enterprise* and *Denver Post* describe the crime and ultimate arrest of two men.

That afternoon the town's streets emptied as residents gathered for a public sale at the Andrew Osborne ranch several miles from Haxtun. Thompson, an employee at the ranch, left the sale and came back to town, where he hung around until two o'clock, when cashier Emil Larson went to lunch, leaving Brunke alone in the bank. Thompson entered the bank brandishing a Savage automatic .32-caliber revolver and ordered Brunke to draw down the window shades.

After pulling down the shades, Brunke made a grab for a revolver kept in a drawer under the counter. Thompson, detecting the move, shot Brunke through the breast. The injured cashier sought refuge in the bank vault where Thompson shot him twice more, once in the neck and once in the temple, before filling his sack and pockets with the contents from the vault and cashier's drawer. Leaving the bank, Thompson strolled east down Fletcher Street to the alley between Colorado and Washington Avenues before turning south, walking the block to the livery stable and mounting his horse. Eyewitness accounts related to Reon Chaney indicate that Thompson rode his horse north to Strohm Street, which was then the DLD Highway,

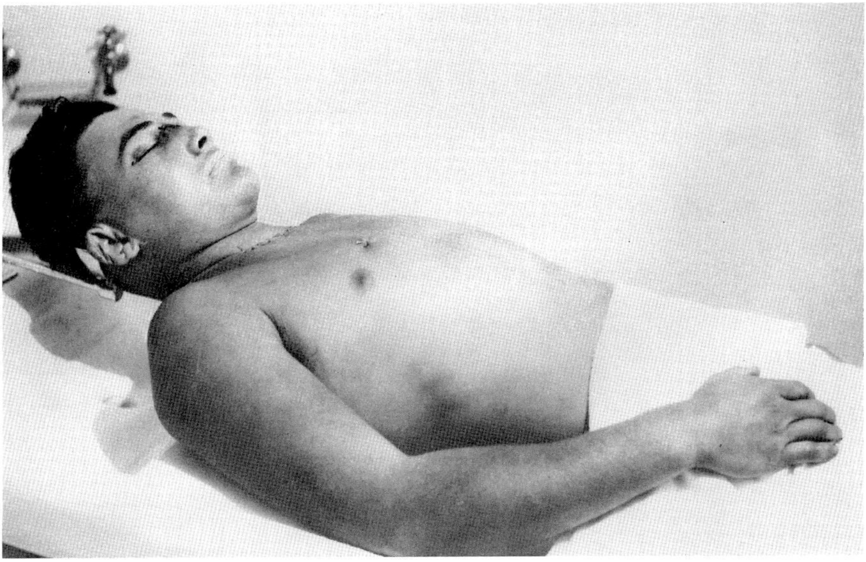

News that robber William Thompson shot and killed the well-liked and handsome young bank cashier John Brunke, *pictured*, during a 1915 hold up at the Farmers State Bank in Haxtun brought near mob violence when a posse captured the accused killer and his accomplice Harry Rose. *Courtesy of Reon Chaney.*

following it west to the edge of town, where it turned north for a mile and then west toward Dailey.

No one heard the shots inside the bank, so the robbery went undetected until around three o'clock, when John Milton Delander and another man entered the bank. A moment later, Manuel Anderson came into the bank, and the three men, hearing heavy breathing coming from the vault, discovered the fatally injured Brunke, who died a few minutes later.

The men sounded the alarm, and the town reacted quickly. Sheriff W.C. Finch organized a posse. D.W. "Walter" Scott, president of the bank, and five other men made chase in the first car, traveling at a high speed, while two other vehicles, all carrying armed men, followed. The posse, spotting Thompson one-half mile ahead, began firing. Thompson rode into a nearby cornfield, turned in his saddle and began returning fire while spurring his horse to a faster speed. As Thompson distanced himself from the pursuing posse, the contents of the sack and his pockets began spilling onto the ground. The fleeing fugitive expanded his lead to a mile before Ralph Hicks, a sharpshooter with a long-distance rifle, shot his horse from under him. Thompson placed his hands in the air and surrendered immediately. News accounts estimated the posse shot hundreds of rounds while Thompson fired fourteen times.

Sharpshooter Ralph Hicks shot bank robber William Thompson's horse from under him with a long rifle as he tried to outrun a posse, but the horse, pictured here, recovered. *Courtesy of Reon Chaney.*

Gaylord McConnell, who worked at the Harry Perry's Belgium horse ranch at the time, recalled the event during a 1988 interview. He was breaking a horse and had ridden it to town. When the posse brought Thompson in, he and Alva Brooks decided to ride out in search of the money. They tracked the blood trail left by Thompson's horse and found money and the revolver that Thompson tossed. Authorities later discovered that thieves stole the gun from a Hot Springs, South Dakota hardware store in October 1914. "The field was so muddy they couldn't drive in by car, but we could get in on horseback," said Gaylord, who noticed immediately that the gun had jammed. "I think if that gun hadn't jammed, someone else might have gotten killed." There was also danger for the "bad guy" that day, he said. "They wanted to hang him out on a telephone pole. It was near mob violence." The crowd calmed when Walter Scott urged them to let the law take its course. John Brunke, twenty-five and unmarried, had worked at the bank for about a year, and people in the community respected him as a "good moral Christian boy." Searchers recovered nearly all of the stolen loot scattered over the field.

Once Sheriff Finch took Thompson into custody, he turned in his accomplice, Charles "Harry" Rose, an employee of the livery stable, stating that Rose provided the gun and then went to the pool hall to "establish an alibi." It was good the mob did not hang Thompson, said Gaylord. "There wouldn't have been anyone left alive to tell." Rose was ready to board a train when Sheriff Finch arrested him.

Soon after their arrest, Thompson and Rose sought a change of venue. An affidavit filed by Naugle and Turman, attorneys for Charles H. Rose, charged prejudice and a fear that the people of the county "would do him violence in the event the trial should result favorably" to him. Thompson's attorneys, Munson and Munson, said the defendant feared that if a jury failed to convict, "he would never get out of the county alive; that a vigilante committee would be gathered together" and he would be "lynched."

William Thompson pleaded guilty in May 1915 and received a life sentence in the State Penitentiary at Canon City. After a jury found Harry Rose guilty, he also received a life sentence.

On April 19, 1933, Governor Edwin C. Johnson pardoned William Thompson after he served eighteen years in prison. A year later in August 1934, Governor Johnson selected Harry Rose, fifty-five, to undergo a serum test "being used in the fight against tuberculosis." A second convicted killer, Lloyd White, also volunteered to take the serum. "In reward for their risking their lives, they will be granted freedom," wrote the *Harvest*.

An attempt by a group of Jeggmen (gypsies) to loot the Haxtun State Bank in April 1924 netted no gain for the robbers but caused sufficient damage to require the bank to call in a safe expert before it could open for business. The robbers gained entrance in the predawn hours by breaking the glass in a rear window of the building. Once inside, they opened the back door so they could carry a " big railroad jack, a spike puller, a spike mall and other tools" into the building, reported the *Harvest*. They used nitroglycerin to blow the outer doors of the safe but only managed to damage the combination. They then tried to remove the combination with the mall and spike puller, but this resulted in "breaking the bolt lever and thus removing all possibility of opening the safe by manipulation of the combination."

Rumors flew on the morning of April 12, 1925, about the hijacking of a "fair-sized poker game" in the basement of the Shirley Hotel by two armed men. Talk around town indicated the gamblers knew the identity of the men who robbed them, but fear of arrest for gambling kept them from revealing the culprits.

Not all robbers wanted money. "There is nothing that adds to the flavor of good, ripe, juicy watermelons than the fact that they have been pilfered from the patch of some farmer who has guarded and tended them carefully all summer," wrote the *Harvest* on September 10, 1925, when nine thieves stole fifteen to twenty watermelons from a field. As they loaded the "fine specimens" in their car, the owner of the patch showed up with a shotgun and commenced firing. Three of the thieves reached the car and managed to make a "rapid getaway, but the other six made a wild dash for the tall corn growing nearby to escape the belching inferno being poured out at them from the rapidly discharging shotgun." The "fusillade of shot" missed all the young men, but most felt it unlikely they would return to the watermelon patch.

For some criminals, justice came swiftly, especially in the case of a robbery that took place at three o'clock on the morning of September 17, 1929, at the Shirley Hotel. Three men woke proprietor Charles O. Olson and requested a room. Afterward, two of the men returned to Olson's door wanting to pay the bill. When Olson turned to make change, the two men followed him into the room and ordered him to hold up his hands. They bound and gagged him, placed him on the bed and instructed him to remain quiet while they ransacked the room and took whatever valuables they could find, including a diamond ring from Olson's finger.

As soon as they left, Olson rolled out of bed and over to the door, where he began pounding with his body and feet. The noise woke other guests in the hotel, who came to his assistance. Olson called Marshal Burt while Deputy Sheriff Roy Brooks, who resided in the hotel, notified Sheriff Frank A. Berger. Fifteen minutes later, Sheriff Berger called to report that he had arrested three men in Holyoke after some difficulty.

The men, driving a Chevrolet coupe, had taken off when they spotted Sheriff Berger. "He over took them and tried to force the car to the curb," wrote the *Harvest*. Although the driver refused to pull over and nearly crashed, Sheriff Berger succeeded in curbing the car and arresting the men. Brooks and Olson drove to Holyoke to identify the men and property, which included about $1,000, a watch and the diamond ring.

CHILDREN DISCOVER BODY NEAR PAOLI

A sadder crime investigated by Sheriff Berger occurred in September 1931, when a group of children found the lifeless body of a young man lying on a road off the DLD Highway, four miles east of Paoli. The body carried no identification, but laundry marks on the clothing and a small fraternity pen gave officers enough clues to identify him as Stanley M. Moore, twenty-one, of Lowell, Michigan, and locate his parents there.

Denver police arrested a suspect several hours later after finding an abandoned Cadillac sedan with a bullet hole in its windshield. Sheriff Berger drove to Denver to assist in questioning the suspect, who identified himself as John Markham, nineteen, of Granite City, Illinois. According to a typed transcript found in court records, Markham admitted stealing the Cadillac from a Kansas City garage. "How did you get that car out of that garage?" asked the officer. "I ran it through the door," Markham responded.

He told officers that he went to Omaha, Nebraska, and then to Lincoln, Nebraska, where he picked up a hitchhiker. The officer pointed at a briefcase and other items they recovered at the time of his arrest and asked Markham if the "boy" had those with him when Markham picked him up. Markham responded, "Yes." He said the hitchhiker indicated he was going to Denver but did not tell him where he was from. The interrogation continued:

> *Officer: How old a boy was this? How tall? How was he dressed?*
>
> *Markham: Oh, I would take him to be twenty or twenty-one. About five foot eight. He was shorter than I am. He had on some knickers, a white shirt and a blue tie; that's about all I remember.*
>
> *Officer: Was he getting inquisitive of you as to how you got the car?*
>
> *Markham: Yes.*
>
> *Officer: Did he discover you had a gun?*
>
> *Markham: No, he didn't know I had a gun.*
>
> *Officer: Was there an argument between you two?*
>
> *Markham: Yes, I tried to get him not to turn me in. I tried to talk him out of that.*
>
> *Officer: When you were near Holyoke, Colorado, and he was driving the car, what did you say to him?*
>
> *Markham: I told him to pull over, and I would drive awhile. When he stopped, I asked him if he still thought he was going to turn me in when we got to Denver; and he wouldn't give me any answer, and I shot him.*

Markham told the officer that he shot Moore in the back of the head with a .45 caliber S&W blue steel pistol. He then got in the front seat, pushed Moore over and drove up the road a short distance before turning onto a back road and driving about a half mile. He removed "all of the identification he could find," pushed the body out of the car and drove to Haxtun where he purchased twenty gallons of gas before continuing on to Denver, where he left the car on Eighteenth Street. He then walked two blocks to the Drake Hotel, where officers later arrested him.

The officer asked how much money Markham took "off this boy you killed?" Markham at first said he did not know, but then admitted he got seven dollars.

A jury found Markham guilty of murder on December 11, 1931, and the court sentenced him to life in prison at Canon City, where he tried to escape in October 1933.

According to the *Harvest*, Markham "developed a knack for photography while in prison" and asked a guard to accompany him to take some pictures at one of the prison farms near Canon City: "Using a dagger as a weapon, Markham forced the guard out of the car and tried to make good his escape." The guard quickly sounded the alarm, and law enforcement captured Markham as he drove into Pueblo a short time later.

The Ku Klux Klan and an Elopement

The Ku Klux Klan made its presence known in Haxtun with the burning of a large cross on North Colorado Avenue and a parade. The burning of the cross in August 1924 caused "considerable speculation" as to the reason, wrote the *Harvest*. "Some advanced the theory that the cross indicated attainment of certain membership by the Klan." Others said that it was a warning to those suspected of "certain infractions" or simply a display for an "appropriate occasion." A few wondered if it was the work of the Klan at all since no one spotted "hooded or robed members" in the area.

The parade took place in April 1925, when Ku Klux Klan members "mysteriously" visited homes in certain sections of town. The parade extended from one end of town to the other, wrote the *Harvest*. "Whether anything was said or done at any of the places where they visited was not learned."

When George Hoschouer, twenty-two, and Helen Baldwin, eighteen, decided to elope on January 30, 1929, they found themselves on the run from Helen's father, Jim Baldwin, who commandeered Buck Wilson and his car to give "chase with a vengeance," wrote the *Harvest*." Jim Baldwin, watching the highway as he stopped to get gas and supplies, spotted the eloping couple and tried to flag them down. The couple, in "no mood for conversation," kept going, heading west. "At this critical time, Buck's car refused to start," so the pursuers "pressed" a second car to continue the chase. They overtook the fleeing pair who "whirled in the road" and headed east.

"After a thrilling chase over pastures and sand creeks" the couple's vehicle "cast a front tire on one of the hairpin turns and was overtaken and forced to the ditch by the pursuers." Following a "heated discussion," between the groom-to-be and the father, the couple promised to return to Fleming. The father, thinking his "prey was helpless," sent his car and driver on their way, walked to a nearby farm and called the sheriff. "But he reckoned not on the resourcefulness of Mr. Hoschouer, for that gentleman pushed his car off the jack, cranked her up, jumped in and was gone!" The father was "left afoot six miles from home to ruminate pensively on the deceitfulness of human nature."

Chapter Seven

CHURCHES, SCHOOLS AND CELEBRATIONS

As settlers took ownership of the High Plains in the 1880s and 1890s, they established schools to educate their children and churches based on various denominational beliefs to nourish spiritual needs. Groups of believers first met in homes and schoolhouses, but as membership grew, they built churches. A few of those early prairie churches continue to serve small congregations while others closed or consolidated in the face of dwindling membership. The social life of these outlying communities centered in those early schools and churches.

On May 25, 2008, 175 people from seven states gathered at the Fairfield Covenant Church to celebrate its 120th anniversary. Following the program on this sun-filled spring day, the crowd drove a short distance to a marble memorial that marks the spot where the Fairfield School once stood. "Those viewing the historical marker can look back upon, not only the paths walked during their time in the Fairfield Community, but also those blazed for them by those pioneers who settled the Fairfield Community," wrote Fairfield historian Mary Ann (Eckman) Ham. "The hardships they endured molded the future, and the foundations they built deserve to be preserved by historical markers so that those who revisit this community down through the years will be reminded of the greatness of these people."

Swedish immigrants settling northwest of Paoli in 1887 organized a school in a granary on Edward Anderson's homestead. A year later, they constructed a sod schoolhouse on Anderson's land and hired Adaline Riffenburg (later Adaline Buckholtz) to teach. They paid Miss Riffenburg, who named the school Fairfield, $25 for the school year, which lasted three months during summer. Records indicate the building materials for the sod schoolhouse—windows, doors, floor and roof—cost about $108.

With the education of the children assured, the settlers moved to caring for the spiritual needs of the community through Bible study and fellowship. Meeting for the first time on December 31, 1888, at Edward Anderson's home, they organized "Fridhem Svenska Missions Forsamling" of Logan County under the leadership of Pastor G. Norseen, a neighboring homesteader. On September 5, 1889, the congregation obtained acceptance from the Evangelical Mission Covenant Church of America and changed the name of the church to the Fairfield Mission Church of Haxtun. Parishioners held church in various schoolhouses until 1894, when they constructed a sod church.

The founders of the Fairfield Evangelical Covenant Church, as shown in minutes written in Swedish until 1927, included Chairman John L. Wilson, Secretary Frank O. Nelson, Cashier Edward Anderson and deacons Nels Swanson, Per E. Person, John Bjorklun and Johannes O. Jacobson. They accepted the Bible as the church's constitution until they could perfect a constitution in "accord with the Bible."

Pastor Norseen promised to preach the gospel at every opportunity, and the membership agreed to help Norseen break sod and plow his land since he would use his own team in getting to services. Nels Swanson served as the first Sunday school superintendent, making sure the children received Bible instructions and followed "the good Swedish traditions" of Midsummer Day picnics and Christmas festivities celebrating Jesus' birth.

The congregation held its first communion on February 10, 1889, at Edward Anderson's schoolhouse, and its first *Julotta*, an early Christmas morning Swedish service, in Pastor Norseen's home on December 25, 1889.

Church leaders asked each member to plant at least one acre of "mission corn" to pay the pastor's salary, but when the corn crop failed that first year, Pastor Norseen received nothing. The church ended the year $4.75 in debt. Pastor Norseen remained with the church until 1892, when he took a pastor's job in Aurora, Nebraska.

Pastor Gustaf F. Palmer came to the Fairfield area in 1890, chaired the church board and took over as pastor in 1892 with a different pay system. Under the new system, the congregation took an offering every three months, with the proceeds going directly to the pastor's salary.

At the annual meeting held on December 29, 1892, members agreed to solicit funds using a subscription list and created two additional offerings, one for foreign mission work and the second, supported by the youth, to send the Sunday school children to Alaska. As a result, the treasurer's report for 1893 showed income of $142.92 and expenditures of $143.12, leaving only a $0.20 deficit for the year.

Around this time, the members decided to build a church north of the cemetery, and the men began work, erecting a three-foot sod wall. However, severe drought in 1893–94 caused some settlers to move away, halting construction.

Despite hard economic times, the settlers continued to support the church, holding services on an irregular basis until Pastor A. Jonson began farming twelve miles south of Haxtun in 1897 and agreed to preach at the church every third Sunday for the occasional offering taken for him. Bengt A. Swedlund filled the pulpit the remaining Sundays until 1899, when Pastor Jonson homesteaded closer to the community and could preach on a regular basis.

The congregation held services in schools and homes around the area until 1905, when the church purchased ten acres of land for $5 per acre from Peter L. Nordquist to build a parsonage and church. The Ladies' Aid Society of the church, formed two years before that in 1903, immediately started a building fund, and the men initiated a subscription list for the same purpose, setting a goal of $600 to construct a parsonage. They reached their goal, completing the parsonage in 1907. Members then raised $1,800 for a church building, which they dedicated on October 17, 1908. Other improvements included the digging of a well and the installation of a windmill.

In the spring of 1892, with forty students in the school, citizens of the Fairfield Community constructed a second sod schoolhouse on property donated by Peter Nordquist. A twenty-foot square wood frame building replaced this second sod schoolhouse in 1900.

Following much discussion and an election in 1916, the school district split into two parts, with the Phillips-Sedgwick county line serving as the division. Since the majority of the students lived in Sedgwick County, officials purchased an acre of land in the center of the district from France Ahnstedt and constructed a two-room schoolhouse with full basement. The district added a two-year high school in 1921, holding classes in the basement, and paid Harry Sprague one hundred dollars per month to drive the students in his canvas-covered truck with its quilt-covered seats. The district later purchased two school buses.

The Fairfield School continued to grow, reaching ninety-three students and four teachers by 1925, when the district added a second level to

Students at Fairfield School posed with the school's two buses in front of the Fairfield School during the 1936–37 school year. Bus drivers Bill Ruch and Carl Eckman stand near the front of their respective busses. *Courtesy of Mary Ann Ham.*

Former Fairfield School students erected this memorial in 2008 to remember teachers and students who passed through the school over the years. Swedish immigrants founded the school in 1887, first holding classes in a granary and then two different sod schoolhouses before the school moved into a wood frame building in 1900. The school consolidated with Haxtun in 1959. *Author photo.*

Trees grow through the broken seats of a merry-go-round and the slipper slide sits solitary and rusted in the playground where students at Fairfield School once played. The school closed after district voters agreed to consolidate with Haxtun in 1959, but they opted to leave the playground equipment as a reminder of the "good old days." *Author photo.*

accommodate three elementary classes, a two-year high school and an auditorium. When the Rural Electric Association brought electricity to Fairfield in 1940, the district installed wiring and lights, dug a well and installed an electric pump.

The school held classes for grades one through ten until 1945, when the district closed the high school and bused the students to Haxtun. Despite the loss of the high school, the school continued to expand, adding a gymnasium in 1954 so students could play basketball without needing to "scoop snow" from the outside court.

Grades six through eight went to Haxtun in 1957, and two years later in 1959, the district voted to consolidate the entire school and transport all of the students to Haxtun.

The school and church served the social needs of the Fairfield Community, recalled Mary Ann Ham: "Memories are vivid of PTA, box socials, school plays, playing coyote, prisoner's base, kick-the-can, football, basketball, softball, banquets, even going to the outhouse in the cold before indoor restrooms were installed in 1952."

The Fairfield church and school remained the center of the community until the spring 1915, when Frank Peterson built the Fairfield Store, later called "Swede Store." Peterson conducted a brisk business, employed several clerks and eventually constructed three additions to his original building.

Over the next few years, other businesses opened in the Fairfield Community, including a blacksmith shop opened by Lewis Cheramy in 1916 north of the store. Lewis's brother Ernest Cheramy made an unsuccessful attempt at running a pool hall and, when that business failed, opened a hardware store. Lewis Cheramy moved his business to Paoli in 1919. When the depression hit, the Fairfield Store closed and Ben Marshall, who sold groceries from the back of his Ford Roadster, moved his business into the building. "He is remembered for his delicious homemade coconut taffy candy," wrote Mary Ann Ham.

After Lewis Cheramy moved to Paoli, Sid Johnson and Joe Anderson opened a blacksmith and auto repair business in the front of the Cheramy building, and Warren Phillips, who also drove the school bus, opened a grocery store and barbershop in the back portion of the building.

The Fairfield Store changed hands three times between 1923 and January 1, 1943, when the United States Government began rationing stamps and requiring grocers to collect them. Owners Mr. and Mrs. Fred Woodham, unwilling to comply, closed the store for the last time.

The Fairfield Covenant Church, which now hosts a congregation of between fifteen and twenty-five worshipers, continues to hold Sunday services each week, a *Julotta* on Christmas and an Easter morning breakfast.

When Peter Lousberg passed through the area south of Fleming in 1894, he found a "barren desert" with "widely-scattered" farms. Writing an English class assignment in 1940, Lila Schlenz explained how her grandfather traveled on to Montana and Canada but, finding those places too cold, returned to Nebraska. During the summer of 1912 "alone in his Jackson," Lousberg traveled again to the "big open spaces" of Colorado. By that time, many of the first settlers, "compelled by crop failures, discouragement and ill success" had lost their land, allowing him to acquire property through "tax title" from Charlie Johnson.

Lousberg retrieved his stock and machinery from Nebraska, constructed a granary to serve as his temporary home and then wrote his sister asking her to bring his children, whose mother had passed away. The letter reached his sister, but her reply encountered confusion when the postal service delivered it to Fleming, California, by mistake. Consequently, Peter Lousberg failed to meet the family when they arrived at Fleming by train. "A kind Mr. Morris offered to take them the eight miles south across the road-less prairie to their father" wrote Lila Schlenz, but the car broke down along the way. As the children waited for Morris to repair the car, they recognized the family dog "straying through the fields" with a horse that also belonged to the family. The dog ran home and "displayed such excitement" that Lousberg followed him, finding his children trailing after the horse.

Six more Nebraska families moved to the area in 1913, "their farms so scattered" that only one house stood between Saint Peters and Sterling and two between there and Haxtun. The few Catholics living in the area traveled to Sterling for Mass once or twice a year.

Around that time, the Platte Valley Land Company advertised the starting of a Catholic settlement south of Fleming, offering land for $25.50 an acre with a stipulation that with every quarter purchased, the buyer sign a $50.00 note to pay toward the construction of a Catholic church. Peter Lousberg donated a corner of his land for the parish site, and a committee made up of Henry Wagner, M.A. Wagner, Ed Stibly, Ed Widner, Frank Pfeiffer and Henry Wilhelm met in Lousberg's granary on April 29, 1913, to discuss plans for building a church.

Lila Schlenz explained the difficulty that task entailed once the lumber arrived at Fleming from Denver. "The men went in two teams to haul it. Again and again the horses gave out," obliging the men to let them rest. "When evening came they were still a far way from home so they let the load stand." One night a storm came up scattering the lumber over the fields.

The congregation finished drilling a well and constructing the building at a cost $1,550 in July 1913 and then added an altar previously used at the Saint Anthony's Church in Sterling. They named the church Saint Peter's after Peter Lousberg. Because of the distance by horse and buggy from Sterling and the Saint Peter's Community, Father Sassu of Sterling offered Mass one day a month for the first year.

In 1914, Reverends Stern and Erger, assistant pastors at Saint Anthony's, alternately celebrated Mass on the first Sunday of each month, taking the train from Sterling to Fleming, where a parishioner would bring them by horse and buggy to the church. The priest on duty would stay at Peter Lousberg's home, celebrate Mass on Sunday morning and attend any planned social events before boarding the train for Sterling on Monday.

Father Peter P. Kluck came to Saint Peter's in January 1919 and immediately began the construction of a rectory. Considered one of the finest in the state, the rectory had electric lights, a water system and finished basement. A 1919 year-end financial statement showed 379 parishioners from 50 families.

Saint Peter's Catholic Church, circa 1919–20, located nine and one-half miles south of Fleming, continues to celebrate Mass each Sunday. Parishioners completed the church building in 1913 and then added a rectory in 1919. *Courtesy of Larry Unrein.*

On February 18, 1920, Father Kluck signed a contract with Frank Brekel to build a school at a cost of $11,100 and an addition to the church for $3,500. Saint Peter's Catholic School opened for classes in the fall of 1920 with eighty-eight students in eight grades. The school added ninth grade classes in September 1933, tenth grade in 1935 and eleventh and twelfth grades in 1936. The last year the school offered high school in 1946, sixteen students received diplomas. Elizabeth Brekel received the school's first diploma in 1937, and the last went to Mildred Lock (Mrs. Julius Wernsman) in 1946.

Governor Ralph L. Carr, on behalf of Logan County resident W.E. Outcalt, filed a lawsuit against the school on September 20, 1949, charging improper use of public funds. At that time, the school operated under an agreement with Logan County School District Forty-three for use of the school building and the Catholic nuns as teachers. In August 1952, Judge George C. Twombly ruled that taxpayer money could not support Saint Peter's School. The school remained open with support from parishioners until 1967, when it closed.

In the spring of 1952, a building committee, made up of Father Halloran, Lawrence Schaefer, John Foxhoven, Albert Brekel, Ed Lock, Henry Burenheide, Charles Boerner, Herman Schlenz and Joe Lousberg, oversaw the planning and construction of parish hall at a cost of $12,000, paid for by fifty parishioners. The Saint Peter's Catholic Church continues to celebrate Mass each Sunday morning, sharing a priest with Haxtun and Holyoke.

SCHOOL DISTRICT EVOLVES FROM SOD TO CONSOLIDATION

At one time, thirty-six school districts served the students of Phillips County with an enrollment of nearly eight hundred students. Each school district operated with a board of education that collected taxes, saw to the construction and maintenance of buildings and hired teachers. Citizens in each county elected a superintendent who evaluated teachers and administrators and reported his or her findings to the state. Voters abolished the office of county superintendent of schools in 1967.

In addition to a schoolhouse, most districts owned a barn to shelter the horses, an outhouse and a shed to hold coal or corncobs used for fuel. Some settlers donated the land while others donated structures. Most of these rural schools offered studies from first through eighth grades. Few students continued their education past the eighth grade, but students who wanted could attend one of the two-year branch high schools located at Highland Center, Amherst, Paoli, Fairfield and Amitie. Haxtun-area students wanting a four-year diploma traveled to Holyoke to attend the Phillips County High School until 1919 when Haxtun opened a high school branch.

Most of these rural schools operated in one room with one teacher who taught grades one through eight, plus handling the daily janitorial work and planning any school programs, including fundraisers to purchase supplies and books.

Genevieve (Reiboldt) Hill recalled a typical day at the West Bryant School for the *Phillips County History*: "As we came through the door into the schoolroom, we saw the big round heating stove sitting on a metal plate to prevent hot coals from falling on the wood floor. There was a coal bucket with a little coal shovel in it sitting in front of the stove. There were rows of desks on either side facing the teacher's big desk. There was a long bench in front of the teacher's desk where students came to sit as the teacher announced the grade and subject."

Haxtun held its first classes in a dugout on the Alice Strohm homestead where the Haxtun Hospital now sits. According to Walter Scott's written memories, which he placed in the cornerstone of the school constructed in 1909, "creating that dugout in the sandy soil was a bit of a problem as the walls kept caving in." The diggers ended up placing boards on all sides of the four-foot deep cavern to hold the soil in place and then extended the sides above the ground high enough for low windows. Scott related that, "education in the early days had a rather low priority." Bliss Hendricks reported only three students two years after the school opened, and Scott recalled an occasion in which the teacher sent two students home for misconduct, leaving one pupil in class that day.

Haxtun Grade School District Eighty-four organized on February 5, 1889, during a meeting held in the office of the Smith & Sons Lumberyard with ten ballots cast, all in favor. Members of the first school board were President S.C Yeager, Secretary E.W. Kendal and Treasurer Washington Strohm. The census that year listed eleven persons of school age.

Sometime before 1908, students moved into a frame schoolhouse that the district moved from south of Haxtun and placed on a lot donated by the Lincoln Land Company. In 1909, board members Walter Scott, George Smith Sr. and Manuel Anderson replaced the frame schoolhouse with a cement block building and paid for it by issuing $2,000 in bonds and collecting the remaining $6,400 in direct taxes. Walter Scott then sold the district land for a playground next to the cement block schoolhouse.

Haxtun School District Eighty-four constructed this block cement schoolhouse in 1909, paying for construction with $2,000 in bonds and $6,400 in direct taxes. Students in first through eighth grades held classes in this building until the district erected a new brick building in 1919. *Courtesy of Reon Chaney.*

When Haxtun constructed its first high school building in 1919, it operated as a branch of the Phillips County system. The county divided in 1953, creating the Haxtun Union High School in the west section of the county. Haxtun Union High School became part of the Haxtun Re-2J School District after reorganization in 1960. *Courtesy of Haxtun School District.*

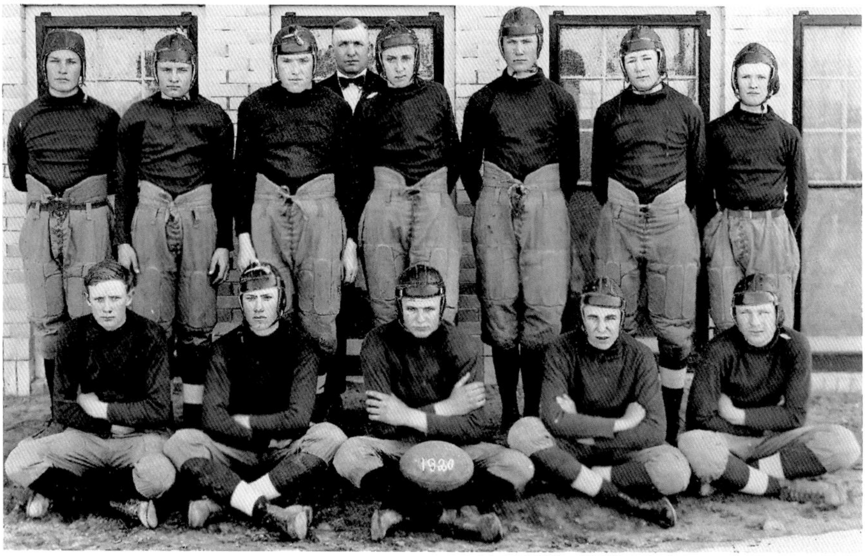

Haxtun High School's first football team played in 1920. Players included *back row left to right*: Harry Gruben, Harold Van Guilden, Carl Nelson, Willis Mitchell, George Kinzie, Fred Peterson and Bernard Barkley; *front row left to right*: Earl L. Chaney, Clifford Fix, Walter Johnson, Everett Beckman, Clyde Van Guilden, William Green (not pictured) and coach Fred Bunger. *Courtesy of Reon Chaney.*

The district expected the two-story building with two rooms on each floor to last for years, but when students soon outgrew it, the first and second grades moved to the Methodist Church while citizens constructed two small bungalows to use for primary grades. By 1919, the census showed 339 students of school age. That year the district erected two brick buildings, one for first through eight grades and a second for high school. The next census listed 400 students. The Haxtun High School graduating Class of 1919 consisted of Iris Intermill and Margert Mitchell.

Haxtun Joint District 7J formed following a special meeting held in the Haxtun High School auditorium in June 1953. Over three hundred representatives from Pumpkin Vine and Good Hope Districts in Logan County and Community Center and Sunbeam Districts in Phillips County attended the meeting to determine whether to join Haxtun Grade School District Eighty-four. The yes vote won, with only forty-two votes against. Later, Phillerado, Plainview and Broadway Districts also joined.

On June 4, 1953, Pumpkin Vine, Good Hope, Community Center and Sunbeam Districts voted to form a joint Haxtun School District Re-2J. The west half of the Phillips County High School District became the Haxtun Union High School District on July 19, 1954. When the Colorado legislature passed laws in 1957 mandating boundary changes slated at creating a more efficient organization of school districts, the number of districts in Phillips County decreased to twelve.

On November 23, 1959, Highland Center, Haxtun Grade School, Fairfield, Buffalo Grass, Paoli, Rockland and Haxtun Union High School joined Haxtun District Re-2J. The reorganized district became legal on January 22, 1960, and voters seated its first board on January 28, 1960. The first board included President Lloyd Skold, Vice-President Robert Grauberger, Secretary Clinton E. Jeffers, Treasurer Charles J. Fryrear, Everett McConnell, John Harms and Donald Wisdom.

The Fleming School District Sixty-nine organized on July 5, 1889, during a meeting held at the Atlas Lumber Company. The first board included John McDonald, A.M. Wilsey and B.W. Crab. The first one-room sod schoolhouse operated four months out of the year. The census listed thirty-six persons of school age.

The district constructed a frame building in 1894. Eventually, the district moved two other one-room schoolhouses from the country, attached them to the first building and hired a second teacher. As farmers left during the drought of the 1890s, many of the small outlying schools closed and consolidated with Fleming. Fleming's first school, built in 1918, operated as a branch of the Logan County High School System.

SETTLERS FOUND WAYS TO CELEBRATE

Even during hard times, settlers on the High Plains found ways to socialize. Neighbors paid visits, often staying for dinner and sleeping over since travel between homesteads and towns took hours or days. The sod house built by Fleming-area homesteader Wilhelm Schmidt included a guest bedroom for travelers from Yuma, New Haven or Rockland who stopped overnight on their way from Sterling. Wilhelm and his wife, Anna, took those opportunities to discuss politics, weather and religion. Rural and town residents gathered to play ball, listen to concerts and participate in a variety of social events.

In 1908, the *E.L. Herald* announced that Haxtun would have a community band, and the *State Herald* explained that Professor C. Clark would lead the sixteen-piece brass band.

When George Irwin "Doc" McCulloch arrived in Haxtun in 1919 with his parents, William and Grace McCulloch, a gazebo sat at the intersection of Colorado Avenue and Fletcher Street where local musical talent gathered to entertain farming families who came to town on Saturday to sell eggs and cream and buy groceries for the coming week.

Circus Day in Haxtun. This photo, taken August 29, 1912, at the intersection of Colorado Avenue and Fletcher Street, shows the Farmers State Bank, *left*, in its first home. This building, constructed in 1904, later suffered fire damage to the rear portion. The Drake Mercantile building replaced all of the buildings on this southwest corner in 1913. The photo shows G.W. Gordon's Bank of Haxtun, which the First National Bank (now town hall) replaced in 1918. The Gordon home was moved a block west to Logan Avenue where it still sits. *Courtesy of Reon Chaney.*

Early gatherings often included a band concert performed by local talent. The Lambert Band organized in 1907 under the direction of Sam and Luella (Monteith) Allen consisted of Jessie Allen, Lennie Allen, Henry Lambert and Crawford Clark. The band played at Corn Festival from 1922 to 1951. Members pictured in this 1950s group include, *back row left to right*: Don Gebhart, Clinton Rice, Jim Baldwin, Henry Lambert and Ray Sipple; *front row left to right*: Leroy Miller, Cora Sipple, Sam Allen, Bobbie Allen, Jessie Gebhart, Alice (Wengert) Holloway and Geraldine Wengert. *Courtesy Town of Haxtun.*

A 1939 Haxtun Municipal Band concert similar to "an old-time minstrel show" included a rendition of "Massa's in the Cold, Cold Ground" by a Dixie quartet and was announced by a promotional flyer. The evening's entertainment ended with the following skit:

> *Inter: Well, Mister Banes, what do you think of the weather? They tell me you are quite a weather prophet.*
>
> *End: Yes sir, and you can take it from me—we're due for a change in the weather.*
>
> *Inter: How do you make that out?*
>
> *End: Just this morning, I was out in the country, and I seen a little sausage crawl out of his hole and look at the sun and then he…*
>
> *Inter: What did you say you saw?*

Most celebrations in the early 1900s and later included baseball games between neighboring communities. The Haxtun men's baseball team won the Interstate League Championship in 1922. Members of the team included True Shannep, father of Inez (Shannep) Dee, who also loved the game. Locals Harold McConnell and Lester Weers played for the team. Note the spelling of "Haxtum" on the flag. The postal service spelled the town's name with an *m* until a group of citizens petitioned for a correction. *Courtesy Town of Haxtun.*

End: A little sausage.
Inter: No, no, you mean a little ground hog.
End: That's what I said.
Inter: No, you said a little sausage.
End: Ha, ha. Aint a sausage a little ground hog?

A program announcing a "Grand 4th of July Fair" in 1893 advertised "Music by Haxtun's String Band of 5 Pieces," a "grand parade," and a "Calathumpian" (a band of noisy discordant instruments). Equestrian events listed "ladies" and "gents" branded pony races, a trotting race and an unbranded stallion race. Other activities included a shotgun shooting match, a tub race on Haxtun Lake and ball games.

Chautauqua offered citizens an opportunity to gather for lectures, music, drama and comedy. Called "the most American thing in America" by President Theodore Roosevelt and "nothing but wind and chaff and the laughter of yokels" by author Sinclair Lewis, the Chautauqua circuit began in 1904 and reached its peak by the mid-1920s.

The Haxtun American Legion sponsored a weeklong *Redpath-Horne Chautauqua* in 1922 that featured the "Boston Entertainers and Oney Fred Sweet," a "fine arts quartet and quartette and entertainment of various varieties, including music, skits and a juggler." The week ended with a children's pageant and the *Jackson Jubilee Singers*. Children paid $0.20 for admission to a single event or $1.00 for a season ticket. Adults paid $0.50 for evening events, $0.35 for an afternoon show and $2.50 for a season ticket.

A different type of entertainment came in December 1924, when around 350 members of the Modern Woodmen of America drill teams gathered in Haxtun for a competition. The *Harvest* reported that the Haxtun drill team captured the silver cup from the Fort Morgan team after which around 300 Woodmen attended a "moving picture" at the Rialto Theater.

Dr. J.D. Cochran opened the Rialto Theater on February 20, 1920, playing to a "packed house" that filled the theater to its capacity of 490. "The opening was something unusual to Haxtun and made one think for a moment of the big city amusement places," reported the *Harvest*. "The Rialto is as classy a theater as anyone could wish for."

Calmar C. McCune recalled growing up in Haxtun with fond nostalgia despite the financial disasters of the late 1920s and early 1930s. Admission to the Rialto Theater was ten cents and Haxtun roared with activity on Saturday nights, he wrote in *Those Were the Days*. "Pretty girls were everywhere and Doc McKnight would treat everyone in the drugstore to an ice cream soda."

The Haxtun American Legion Fred C. Leman Post sponsored the Fourth of July celebration in 1922, hosting a concert by the Haxtun Municipal Band, ball games, free outdoor acts, a water fight between the Haxtun and Holyoke fire departments and bronco busting. The evening included prize fighting between Lester "Skinny" Fitzgerald of Haxtun and Young Jim Flynn of Denver. A dance in the Suhl Garage with music by a six-piece orchestra followed a "grand display of fireworks."

Haxtun boxer Lester "Skinny" Fitzgerald "attracted the attention of promoters in practically every appearance he has made," bragged the *Harvest* in 1922. Fitzgerald won a knockout decision against Ray Kous for the welterweight championship of Northeastern Colorado in July 1922.

The Fred C. Lewman Post organized on April 12, 1921, during a meeting held at the Shirley Hotel. The membership grew to nineteen by the end of the first year and increased to forty-two by November 1922. The group began plans to erect a "commodious home" (Legion Hall) the following summer. The idea materialized when the Haxtun State Bank donated

Inez (Shannep) Dee, *fourth from left*, inherited her father's love of baseball and played for a number of teams, including the Haxtun Coop team in 1935–36. She said the team took many honors and left the players with fond memories before it broke up after the girls left to get married. *Courtesy Town of Haxtun.*

a lot in September 1925. Members then formed the American Legion Corporation and launched a drive to sell certificates to pay for the building. The Haxtun American Legion Hall opened on November 25, 1925, when members started a fire in the new heating plant. "Somehow that first fire in the new building seemed to give the impression of a habitable home," wrote the *Harvest*.

That morning, the community joined members as they held a dedication followed in the evening with a "big house-warming" dance with Raymond Kane and his orchestra furnishing the music. After the dance, the building closed while the painters, plumbers, cement men and decorators completed the work, which included "nine coats of dressing" to finish the floor in the dance hall. The Legion Hall saw many forms of entertainment over the years, including a minstrel show in March 1928 and a "Big Boxing Show" in May 1929.

Nearly every community found reasons to hold festivals. Paoli held its first annual Harvest Jubilee and Rodeo in August 1929, drawing a crowd of between five thousand and seven thousand persons. Vendors sold hotdogs, and Perry Ballantine and his wild horses performed with only one mishap. "One of the riders was kicked after he was unseated by his mount," wrote the *Harvest*. "There [were] some unusually good horses, and there were some riders good enough to ride them."

Dailey drew a large crowd for its annual Dailey Community Day on September 21, 1935, when the celebration opened with a horseshoe tournament. Contests for boys and girls included foot races, a bicycle race, shoe scramble, nail driving and a rolling pin contest. Events in the afternoon included a pony race and two softball games between the Haxtun and Dailey girls and the Dailey and Paoli boys.

Fleming held its first Fall Festival in 1931. The day included a showing of the areas gardening successes from growing to canning plus other handmade crafts, races for the children and a kids' rodeo with events like goat tying and cow-pie bingo.

Fleming held "cornhusking" contests for nine years before Haxtun decided to join the fun in 1934. That year, members of the Haxtun Commercial Club sponsored a Phillips County corn-shucking contest after representatives of the Fleming Commercial Club indicated that five counties in northeast Colorado planned to host contests. Fleming held its twelfth-annual cornhusking contest on October 22, 1937, with a daylong celebration.

Haxtun's Corn Festival started in 1922 after the *Harvest* ran an editorial in August pointing out that many towns around the state held celebrations honoring the products each produced. "Rocky Ford has its watermelon day; Glenwood Springs its strawberry day; Grand Junction its peach day" wrote the *Harvest*. "Therefore, nothing could be more fitting than that Haxtun should observe corn day." A few weeks later, the newspaper announced that the Haxtun Corn "Carnival" would happen due to the "demand of a majority of the residents of this town," and all agreed it should become an annual event.

Planners decided to build a "big picnic feed with a corn menu" into the day, with cornbread, corn muffins, old-fashioned corn pone and hoecakes (pancakes made with flour and corn meal). They also served "barbecued beef, mutton and pork and baked and fried chicken; coffee with real cream along with jams, jellies and preserves." Activities throughout the day included ballgames, fireworks and automobile races. The Haxtun Municipal Band played all day, and dancing went into the night.

Early in the 1930s, the town ceased holding the event because poor crop production and hard economic times left little to celebrate. However, in September 1932, the Haxtun Commercial Club sponsored a Farmers' Day that drew around 1,500 people. The lunch served at the Haxtun Town

Hall included cheese and meat sandwiches, fruit, cookies and coffee. A few brought their own lunches and held a picnic at the Haxtun Park. Stores in town closed for the day so owners and employees could join their "farmer friends in games and recreation of all kinds," reported the *Harvest.*

The Haxtun Commercial Club revived the Haxtun Corn Festival in October 1935. That year, a delegation from Holyoke met with the Haxtun Commercial Club to offer support in "staging the event." The *Harvest* gave no specifics for entertainment but reported, "Prizes will be given for every product of the farm and a large display of crops and vegetables grown in this community." The September 16, 1935 edition of the *Harvest* estimated that "farmers and their families from four counties in northeastern Colorado are expected to attend Haxtun's Tenth Corn Festival," which the Commercial Club arranged "solely for the entertainment of the farmers."

Chapter Eight

THE WOMEN AND MEN WHO TAMED HAXTUN

Hundreds of men and women built the town of Haxtun and turned the wild prairie into farmland. Some left their mark before moving on. Others stayed, leaving descendants who continue to live in the area. This history considers only a few of those truly brave pioneers.

Kate Charlotte Fletcher and Alice Constance Strohm each homesteaded land that became the original town site of Haxtun. Kate Fletcher stayed in the area, married and left a legacy infused with the pioneer spirit of hard work and endurance. Alice Strohm remained single and returned to metropolitan society but not before writing her own part of Haxtun's history.

The daughter of Samuel S. and Sarah (Stringer) Strohm, Alice Strohm was born on December 21, 1857, in Pelham Township, Welland County Ontario, Canada. She immigrated to the United States in 1864 and became a naturalized citizen in 1869. By the 1880 U.S. Census, she lived in Seward County, Nebraska, with her sister Leora (Strohm) Waterman. The Nebraska agriculture census of 1885 listed Alice Strohm as a schoolteacher.

Kate Fletcher and Samuel Strohm received patents on neighboring sections of land in Phillips County on June 6, 1889. Alice Strohm received a patent on land south of Kate Fletcher on July 1, 1889.

Kate Fletcher was born November 24, 1860, at Fairfield, Iowa. The family migrated to Kansas in the 1800s, but drought and grasshopper plagues caused the rest of the family to return to Iowa while Kate headed to Colorado with friends in a covered wagon.

Alice Constance Strohm, daughter of Samuel and Sarah (Stringer) Strohm, homesteaded 160 acres of land that she later sold to the Lincoln Land Company for platting part of the original Town of Haxtun. Strohm, who petitioned for a post office and served as Haxtun's first postmaster, received her land patent on July 1, 1889. *Courtesy of Connie Lawrence.*

A May 2005 story in *Palouse Magazine*, a publication of the Whitman County Iowa Library, reported that Sarah Strohm told her great-grandchildren that she traveled to Colorado by covered wagon. The exact date the Strohm family arrived in Colorado remains uncertain, but an April 21, 1888 news item in the *Dayton Chronicle*, a newspaper published in Columbia County, Washington, indicates that Samuel and Sarah Strohm, three sons and a Charles Delzell left Colorado around that date. A June 15, 1889 item from the *Chronicle* reported: "Washington Strohm, eldest son of Mr. and Mrs. Samuel Strohm, died Tuesday in Haxtun, Colorado."

The remainder of the family apparently left Haxtun after Washington's death. The *Chronicle* relates that Juliet Strohm arrived in Dayton from Haxtun on Saturday, June 29, 1889, and that her brother, James Strohm, and sister, Alice Strohm, moved from Haxtun to Dayton on July 27, 1889.

Alice and her sister, Juliet, traveled by ship to Munich, Germany, in August 1893 and returned in August 1894. The next news of Alice Strohm appears on April 17, 1897, when the *Chronicle* reported that she was "slowly recovering from injuries" received when five passenger cars on the Oregon Short Line jumped the tracks in Idaho.

Although she spent a short time in Haxtun, Alice Strohm left a historic mark. She petitioned the postmaster general on August 9, 1887, requesting the establishment of a post office at what would later be the town of Haxtun. The postal service established the Haxtun Post Office on April 25, 1888, naming Alice C. Strohm its first postmaster.

A number of reports indicate that Alice Strohm wanted to name the new town "Lillydale" or "Lily Dale," but a Mr. Emerson, who worked for the Lincoln Land Company, named the town Haxtun after a New York town on the Hudson River. Alice's sister, Juliet, married Samuel Emerson, a "well-educated man" and the grandson of Samuel Delucenna Ingham, secretary of the treasurer under Andrew Jackson, according to Connie Lawrence, a Strohm descendant. Whether Samuel Emerson was the Mr. Emerson who named Haxtun is unknown.

Alice was teaching at Horace Mann School in Spokane, Washington, by 1929 but moved to Baltimore, Maryland, to live with her sister, Juliet, around 1935 after their mother died. She lived there until her death in 1937.

A warranty deed filed at the Phillips County Courthouse shows that Kate C. Fletcher received $1,176.75 from Lincoln Land Company on February 8, 1888, for her homestead. She then purchased a homestead north of Haxtun and married Albert Edwards on January 28, 1894.

Albert Edwards, the son of David and Rebecca Edwards, was born on March 8, 1867, in Kirksville, Missouri. He spent two years working on the

Albert and Kate (Fletcher) Edwards with son Charles (circa 1898–1900). Kate Fletcher homesteaded land that later became part of the original Town of Haxtun. *Courtesy of Tom Edwards.*

railway line between Kansas City, Missouri, and Ottumwa, Iowa, and then moved to Illinois for a couple years before arriving in the Haxtun area in 1891. He homesteaded land adjoining Kate Fletcher's and supplemented his farm income working in logging in the Colorado Mountains. Albert and Kate combined their homesteads and joined their buildings to make a home after they married. Through hard work, they created one of the most successful ranches in the area.

Kate (Fletcher) Edwards took an active role in the early religious history of the community, wrote the *Harvest* after her death. She taught a Sunday school class in the old stone schoolhouse and "shared with her friends and neighbors the hardships of the pioneering days." Centurion Irene Livingston recalls Kate (Fletcher) Edwards as a "tiny woman who worked hard."

Albert and Kate Edwards remained on the homestead until Kate's death on January 5, 1942. Albert then moved to Wanatchee, Washington, where he lived until 1955. He spent his final year in Haxtun, where he died in 1956.

The Fletcher-Edwards homestead passed first to the couple's only son, Charles Elmer Edwards, and then to Charles's son, Rex Phillip Edwards. Rex's son, Thomas Neal, and his wife, Shawn (Prussman) Edwards, currently live on the homestead.

Albert and Kate (Fletcher) Edwards at their homestead in 1939. After selling her homestead to the Lincoln Land Company for the Haxtun town site, Kate Fletcher purchased a second homestead and later married neighboring homesteader Albert Edwards. The two combined their homesteads and developed one of the most successful ranches in the area. *Courtesy of Tom Edwards.*

A bench commemorating Haxtun's first town clerk, John Milton Delander, sits outside the Haxtun Town Hall, a gift from the John F. Delander Trust, which gave the town $25,000 in memory of John M. Delander in 2010. Another gift of $25,000 went to the Haxtun School District for scholarships. The town's memorial came in two checks, one for $5,000 to use for lighting and new furnishings in the town hall and a second to purchase lighting for the main street improvement project. The town purchased the bench, chosen by the family, to place in front of the town hall to acknowledge the gifts.

The son of Swedish immigrants, John Milton Delander was born May 28, 1881. He completed his studies at Augustana College in Rock Island, Illinois, and business school in Colorado Springs and then worked for a time in Atlanta, Georgia, and Denver before moving to Haxtun sometime before 1909. After arriving in Haxtun, he opened his business as a real estate broker and insurance agent. Since he spoke Swedish, he assisted many of the immigrants in the Swedish community of Fairfield in their business

John Milton Delander, Haxtun's first town clerk, at his desk in his real estate and insurance office at the corner of Colorado Avenue and Raymond Street. Circa 1916. *Courtesy of Scott Williams.*

dealings, said his daughter, Marguerite Baker, a 1934 graduate of Haxtun High School.

John M. Delander married Dola M. Hallgren of Holdrege, Nebraska on December 15, 1912, in Haxtun. Dola taught elementary grades in Haxtun Schools for sixteen years and served on the Haxtun Board of Education.

John M. Delander also worked part-time editing the *E.L. Herald* and helped organize and fund the First National Bank on July 23, 1917. He moved to Denver in 1941, where he continued to work as a real estate broker until he retired in 1951. He died on October 23, 1976.

In 1959, the Town of Haxtun celebrated its fiftieth anniversary with a parade during Corn Festival that honored the first town officials. They included Mayor Harvey O. McNichols, trustees Nels Herbert Bentson, Kinzy Oscar Dannells, Olin Horton Hilland, John T. Monteith, Rolland E. Shearer and George Smith Sr., Marshal Charles J. Johnson, Town Clerk John M. Delander, Clerk Pro-tem Oscar W. Lohn Sr., Treasurer George W. Gordon, City Attorney George B. Spencer and Health Officer Dr. W.H. Keesee. Only Delander and Lohn participated in the parade.

Harvey O. McNichols was born in Iowa in 1881. Calling himself "Haxtun's Hardware Man," he owned and operated the H.O. McNichols store. According to U.S. census records, he moved to Long Beach, California, and later Greeley, Kansas.

Olin Horton Helland, a druggist and the son of William and Gilbert Holland, was born in Wyoming in 1883. He came with his family to Colorado in 1886, where they homesteaded and lived in a dugout three miles east of Holyoke. Olin married Molly Kelly in Holyoke on May 6, 1907, and later moved to Otis. He died in Douglas County on September 8, 1944.

Nels Herbert Bentson gave generously to the Haxtun community, according to a *Harvest* article written after he died on Sunday, May 8, 1929, at the age of forty-five. Born in Billesholm, Sweden, on March 16, 1884, Nels Bentson immigrated to America in 1885 with his parents, who used their Swedish name Sorenson. The family lived in Oakland, Nebraska, for a time before homesteading in the Fairfield Community in 1887.

At the age of eighteen in 1902, Nels Bentson became the first clerk to work in Manuel Anderson's store. He later opened his own mercantile business, which he operated for seventeen years. After selling his store, he engaged in real estate, insurance and banking. In addition to serving on the town council, he served on the school board and church board.

Nels Bentson married Haxtun teacher Bertha Riley in Gothenberg, Nebraska, on August 11, 1914. "The name N.H. Bentson is prominently identified in the community with every movement that made for the betterment of the town, the church, the school, the home, and he has always been numbered among its substantial citizens," wrote the *Harvest* at the time of his death.

John T. Monteith, the son of John W. and Lucinda Monteith, was born in Rockport, Missouri, on November 2, 1854, but the family later moved to Henderson, Illinois, and Monroe, Iowa. He married Adaline Gladson in 1876. They moved to Haxtun in 1905. After Adaline died in 1928, John remained in Haxtun, living with his daughter and son-in-law, John and Luella Allen, until his death on April 29, 1941, at the age of eighty-six.

Pioneer rancher and farmer George Carl Smith Sr. suffered a stroke that caused his death on February 1, 1932. "There are few men left in the Haxtun country who were so solidly identified with the early development of the community," wrote the *Harvest*. "He came here at a time when farming was in its infancy and settlers depended largely upon cattle and sheep for their livelihood." George Smith was born in Nashville, Tennessee, in 1857. At the age of twenty-one, he headed to Indian country, where he lived for four years before moving to Eaton and marrying Sarah Garwood. "A progressive pioneer type, Mr. Smith followed the westward progress of early American frontiersmen until he finally made his home in Haxtun country," said the *Harvest.* The paper called him a "rugged type pioneer that made the early settlement of the frontier possible."

Marshall Charles "Charlie" J. Johnson immigrated to the United States from Sweden at the age of sixteen and filed a homestead south of Haxtun near his parents. He later worked in meat markets in Holyoke, Holdrege, Nebraska and Loveland, where he met and married his wife, Lizzie, in 1896. They returned to Charlie's homestead, where they lived until Charlie, Lizzie and their daughter Elvira moved into Haxtun.

After Charlie served as Haxtun's first marshal, he collaborated with Oscar W. Lohn Sr. to open the C.J. Johnson Market and Royal Café, later buying Lohn's share. According to Velma Baylor, writing in *Those Were the Days*, Charlie's bologna and headcheese were "food fit for the gods." Lizzie established her own reputation in photography. After a fire destroyed the market in August 1919, Charlie and Lizzie built the Shirley Hotel. Charlie and Lizzie celebrated sixty years of marriage before Charlie died in 1959.

Oscar W. Lohn Sr. worked as a real estate broker and helped organize the Haxtun State Bank in 1919. He was born at Joliet, Illinois, on February 28, 1876, but moved to Loomis, Nebraska, with his parents in 1885. He then moved to Colorado, settling in Haxtun in 1901. He served as the second elected mayor of Haxtun before moving to Paoli, where he was actively involved in the development of that community both as a member of the Paoli Commercial Club and as mayor. He died while serving as mayor of Paoli on November 3, 1961.

Born in New York in 1862, George W. Gordon moved to Kearney, Nebraska, with his parents in 1879. He and his brother-in-law, Axel Chinndgren, opened a hardware store in Julesburg in 1886, erecting the first building in that town. He then moved to Chappell, Nebraska, where he operated a flour and feed store and met his wife, Elizabeth Gertrude Babcock. They married on July 4, 1888. The couple homesteaded and operated businesses in a number of Nebraska communities before coming to Haxtun in March 1906. He founded the Bank of Haxtun in 1906, sold his shares to the investors of the First National Bank in 1917 and then helped start the Haxtun State Bank in 1919.

George W. Gordon died of a self-inflicted shotgun wound on February 29, 1944. "Mr. Gordon undoubtedly weakened by his age and a long illness, and tired and weary during a period of melancholy, took a gun from a tenant's apartment at the Shirley Hotel building and went into the building where he was found," wrote the *Harvest* on March 3, 1944. The building still stands across the alley west of the Shirley Hotel. "Mr. Gordon assisted in a financial way with the early development of this territory, and witnessed its development into a more prosperous farming country," wrote the *Harvest*. "He stood as a financial strength during the leaner years and aided many to weather those years."

Dr. W.H. Keesee came to Haxtun in 1908 and, for a time, was the only practicing physician in "this section of the county," wrote the *Harvest*. Dr. Keesee died during a stay at the Saint Thomas Hotel in Denver. He was "well or better known than any other man in the Haxtun country and many were proud to claim him as a friend."

HAXTUN'S NEWSPAPER PIONEERS

Dean Schuman of Sterling started Haxtun's first newspaper, the *Haxtun E.L. Herald* on December 18, 1907, as a weekly edited and published by the Haxtun Epworth League, an organization connected to the Methodist Episcopal Church. Delvan W. Gee, formerly with newspapers in Meeker, Granite, Leadville and Steamboat Springs, started the *Haxtun Harvest* on March 13, 1919. In July 1921, Adolph A. Herzberg and Tom Crist joined Gee at the *Harvest*.

A Missouri native, Tom Crist tried homesteading south of Haxtun but soon relinquished his claim to work at the *Holyoke Enterprise*. He later worked at the *Sterling Advocate*, the *Rocky Mountain News* in Denver and the *Boulder Farmer & Miner*.

Born in Lebanon, Tennessee, on May 3, 1895, Leslie Taylor served in the United States Army during World War I and then moved Haxtun in 1921, taking a job at the *E.L. Herald*. Taylor and Crist quit their jobs a month later and sojourned to Wray, Denver and Limon looking for a newspaper to purchase. They met with little success due to a lack of funds. Arriving back in Haxtun in April 1922, Taylor returned to his job at the *E.L. Herald* while Crist stayed in Denver.

When the editor of the *Harvest* quit the following June, the owner asked Taylor to publish both the *E.L. Herald* and the *Harvest*, which he did, asking Crist to return to Haxtun to help him. The two purchased both newspapers and combined them into the *Harvest* a few months later.

Crist served as editor of the *Harvest* until he sold his interest to Taylor to take an appointment as Haxtun postmaster on June 14, 1934. He continued as postmaster until his death from pneumonia on October 8, 1949.

Active in politics and concerned about the welfare of his community, Crist served as a member of the Phillips County Relief Committee, working long hours during the Great Depression. Also active in politics, Taylor served as relief administrator for Phillips and Sedgwick Counties in 1934 and 1935, on the selective service board for over thirty years and won election to the represent Phillips and Sedgwick Counties in the thirty-first General Assembly of the Colorado House of Representatives in 1936.

President Harry S. Truman appointed Leslie Taylor postmaster in 1951, a position he held while publishing the *Harvest* until 1965. On October 29, 1975, Taylor announced his intent to suspend publication of the *Harvest* with that edition and to send refunds to subscribers. He stated that he wanted all subscribers to accept their refunds: "No gifts, please." Taylor died on October 27, 1978.

Chapter Nine

LESSONS IN SURVIVAL

A decreasing rural population as farming operations grew in size coupled with paved roads and faster automobiles that took residents to larger towns to shop caused businesses in small rural trade centers like Haxtun and its neighboring communities to shrink. While Haxtun's population remains near one thousand, the same as it has for over one hundred years, the business community on Colorado Avenue no longer thrives. That does not equate to a dying town, however. These days, entrepreneurs run businesses out of their homes, the community continues to support a strong medical system—with a hospital, extended-living center and medical clinic—and agriculture fuels a strong economy.

Grainland Cooperative, a consolidation of farmers' cooperatives, is one of the largest employers in the area. Another large employer, Haxtun Schools, with its growing student body, receives high marks on state standard testing, a result of the community and school working together to raise well-adjusted and well-educated young people. That tradition of working together has brought rural and town residents together numerous times throughout Haxtun's history.

When the Haxtun State Bank closed on October 31, 1942, leaving the town without a bank, a group of local investors came forward to open the Haxtun Community Bank on February 19, 1944. Stockholders, headed by Mayor Ralph L. Scott, numbered over one hundred.

When citizens wanted a hospital in the 1960s, a group canvassed the community selling stock in $100 and $200 increments to form a stock company to open the Haxtun Community Hospital. A few years later, voters "overwhelmingly" passed a $400,000 bond question for construction of a new hospital building, which the Haxtun Hospital District completed in 1965. The new building housed a sixteen-bed hospital and a seventeen-bed nursing home. The district came back to the voters in 1986, 1990, 1992, 2004 and 2008, seeking help to expand the facility or support to keep it open. The voters said yes each time.

The dream of a new Haxtun Community Center, driven by Haxtun mayor Gay McDaniel, became reality at an open house held on Saturday, July 24, 1999—after voters gave their approval on April 7, 1998, allowing the town to borrow $300,000 and to enact a half-cent sales tax to pay the debt. Voters reinforced that approval in 2000 by repassing the half-cent sales tax to pay for maintenance. As her final act leaving office in April 2008, Mayor McDaniel burned the $300,000 note, marking it paid. Haxtun's first female mayor, Gay (Goddard) McDaniel, the granddaughter of pioneers, took her oath of office as mayor on April 20, 1992 after serving for twelve years as a council member.

When members of Haxtun's Vision Committee decided that Haxtun needed first-rate signs to welcome visitors entering town limits on Highway 6, they raised the needed funding and then enlisted the help of local volunteers Winston Ham and Doyle Orcutt to construct the redwood backboards that contain the vinyl lettering. The first sign went up on the west edge of town in March 2000. Two years later, with financial help from the Haxtun Booster Club and the Haxtun Chamber of Commerce, the group seated a matching sign to welcome travelers from the east.

The Haxtun Volunteer Fire Department (HVFD) began efforts to replace its outdated conglomerate of buildings in September 2005. The thirty-member department painted the replica of a thermometer on a sign in front of the fire hall and began an intensive effort to raise the $750,000 needed to build a new emergency services building to house the police department, fire department and ambulance service. By July 2007, they raised $219,820 in cash and in-kind donations. In April 2008, HVFD learned the Colorado Department of Local Affairs funded their request for a $400,000 Energy/Mineral Impact Assistance grant, and HVFD held its first event, hosting Santa Claus, in the new building in December 2008.

Conversations on the need for daycare in Haxtun began in June 1997, but it took a dozen years and a group of young, hard-working mothers to make it happen. The Haxtun Community Childcare Center held its open house on September 6, 2011.

Despite the frustrating number of buildings along Colorado Avenue that nonresidents use for storage, residents of Haxtun passed a one-percent sales tax that allowed the town to borrow $750,000 to revitalize Haxtun's downtown area. The tax passed by a margin of 220–86 on April 6, 2010.

Following the first phase of the project in 2010, a one-block area from Highway 6 west to the railroad tracks, Haxtun's Visions Committee raised money and in-kind labor to erect a welcome meridian to greet visitors as they turn north off Highway 6. The town finished the main-street project, complete with trees and benches, all donated by citizens, in time for a ribbon cutting that opened the Haxtun Corn Festival on September 29, 2012.

Traditionally, the citizens of Haxtun, flanked by those who live on the farms surrounding the town, form coalitions, donate time and money and even tax themselves to build or save the facilities needed to retain a strong community.

Wayne C. Lee related in his book that when a reporter asked Scotty Philip why he wanted to preserve the buffalo, he replied:

> *I have watched the buffalo under all conditions of their life. I have discovered many interesting things about the animal. I used to wonder how the comparatively delicate calves could withstand the terrible blizzards, which occasionally sweep over our country, but now I know how it is done. When a storm comes, the buffalo form themselves into a triangle with the bulls along the sides—the boss bull standing at the apex facing the storm. Then the cows arrange themselves inside the lines of the bulls and in the well-protected center, the calves and yearlings find their place. The mass is crowded well together into a warm and living whole, and even in the case of the outline of bulls, only one side of any animal is presented to the blizzard. The herd will maintain this triangle so long as the storm lasts, and they are able safely to weather a storm that would kill our native cattle. If man wants to get a fine lesson in the advantage of "standing together" he need only watch the buffalo herd in stormy weather.*

That same spirit of "standing together" allowed the pioneers to tame the High Plains, and it still happens in rural areas and small towns across America today.

BIBLIOGRAPHY

Branch, E. Douglas. *The Hunting of the Buffalo*. Lincoln: University of Nebraska Press, 1962.

Christman, Abigail, Deon Wolfenbarger, and Claudia Woodman. *The Legacy of the New Deal on Colorado's Eastern Plains*. Denver: Colorado Preservation, Inc., Colorado Historical Society, Denver Public Library, 2008.

Conklin, Emma Burke. *A Brief History of Logan County, Colorado*. Denver, CO: Welch-Haffner Printing Company, 1928.

Davies, Henry Eugene. *Ten Days on the Plains*. Vol. 2. Edited by Paul Andrew Hutton. Dallas, TX: Southern Methodist University Press, 1985.

Fairfield Covenant Church Centennial Committee. *Fairfield Covenant Church Haxtun, Colorado 1888–1988*. Haxtun, CO: Fairfield Covenant Church, 1988.

Fleming Historical Society. *Memories of Our Pioneers*. Iowa Falls: General Publishing and Binding, 1971.

Fleming Historical Society and Paul Lambert, curator. *Our Pioneer Heritage, Fleming, Colorado*. Alden, IA: Graphic Agri-Business, 1981.

Fort Sedgwick Historical Society. *Jules? Who?* Fort Sedgwick Historical Society Archives. Julesburg, CO.

Hafen, LeRoy R., and Ann Hafen. *The Colorado Story: A History of Your State and Mine*. Denver, CO: Old West Publishing Company, 1953.

Ham, Mary Ann (Eckman). *Fairfield School Through the Years*. Haxtun, CO: PAK Enterprises, 2008.

Haxtun Centennial Committee. *Haxtun 100 Years: A Small Town with a Big Heart*. Haxtun, CO: Town of Haxtun, 2009.

Haxtun Town Council. Minutes. July 20, 1909–December 17, 1928.

Jones, James R. "Jim," and Russ Collman. *Sterling, Colorado: Crossroads on the Prairie*. Denver, CO: Sundance Books, 2000.

Kugler, Deb, ed. *Phillips County History*. Dallas, TX: Curtis Media Corporation, 1993.

Lee, Wayne C. *Scotty Philip: The Man Who Saved the Buffalo*. Caldwell, ID: Caxton Printers, Ltd., 1975.

Lincoln Land Company. Town file documents. Microfilm. Nebraska Historical Society.

Morris, Elizabeth Ann. *Report on Archaeological Investigation at Schlachter Sites near Holyoke, Colorado*. Department of Anthropology. Colorado State University. Fort Collins, CO, 1987.

Palouse Magazine. Whitman County: Whitman County Iowa Library, May 2005.

Paoli Commercial Club (Chamber of Commerce). Minutes. 1926–1931.

Paoli Town Council. Minutes. September 22, 1930–September 11, 1984.

Phillips County Historical Society. *Those Were the Days*. Centennial ed. Phillips County, CO: privately printed, 1988.

———. *Those Were the Days: Reminiscences of Early Days by Early Settlers.* Holyoke, CO: Holyoke Enterprise Printing Co., 1973.

Schlenz, Lila. "Saint Peter's Colorado." Paper for English class. Circa 1940s.

Sterling Centennial Committee. *Sterling Colorado Centennial, 1884–1994: Logan County Families*. Sterling, CO: Taylor Publishing, Co., 1984.

Sutton, E.S. *Southwest Nebraska and the Republican River Valley Tributaries*. N.p.: E.S. Sutton, 1983.

United States Postal Service. *History of Phillips County Post Offices 1887–1988: 101 Years.* N.p.: privately published: 1988.

Unrein, Mary. *Early History of St. Peter's Catholic Church.* N.p.: privately published, 2012.

Wells, Dale. *Logan County Ledger*. Sterling, CO: Logan County Historical Society, 1976.

Whitman, Walt. *Complete Prose Works: Specimen Days and Collect, November Days and Good Bye My Fancy*. Kindle ed. N.p., 2005.

Wilkins Trivis E. *Colorado Railroads: Chronological Development*. Boulder, CO: Pruett Publishing Company, 1974.

Newspapers

Dayton Chronicle. Columbia County, WA, 1888–89
Haxtun E.L. Herald. Haxtun, CO, 1907–08
Haxtun Harvest. Haxtun, CO, 1919–75
Haxtun Herald. Haxtun, CO, 1975–2012
Holyoke Enterprise. Holyoke, CO, 1915–18
Logan County News. Holyoke, CO, 1887–88
State Herald. Holyoke, CO, 1888–1935

Websites

Indians.org.
www.ancestry.com.
www.archives.gov.
www.cogenweb.com.
www.coloradodot.info/programs/environmental/archaeoloy-and-history/highways-to-the-sky/highwaystothesky.pdf/view.
www.cwi.colostate.edu.
www.eHow.com.
www.farmcreditbank.com.
www.fsa.usda.gov.
www.gatewayno.com.
www.historyplace.com.
www.ksha.org.
www.mesalek.com/colo.
www.nebraskahistory.org.
www.nebraskastudies.org.
www.nndb.com.
www.sterlingcolo.com.
www.utahrails.net.
www.weldcounty150.org.

INDEX

D

E

F

G

H

N

O

P

Q

R

S

T

U

W

ABOUT THE AUTHOR

Jean Gray is an award-winning journalist with over thirty years of experience working in rural community newspapers. She earned writing awards for feature stories, editorials and news coverage. A strong advocate for the First Amendment, the Colorado Freedom of Information Council awarded Gray the Jean Otto Friend of Freedom Award in 2002, and the Colorado Press Association named her Newspaper Publisher of the Year in 2005.

A Kansas transplant, Gray continues to live and work in Colorado, where she enjoys searching for stories that speak of the history of people and places. Additional information from Gray can be found at her website, http://cjeangray.wordpress.com.